Finding Spiritual Direction

Douglas D. Webster

The Challenge & Joys of Christian Growth

foreword by Eugene H. Peterson

INTERVARSITY PRESS
DOWNERS GROVE, ILLINOIS 60515

InterVarsity Press is the book-publishing division of InterVarsity Christian Fellowship, a student movement active on campus at hundreds of universities, colleges and schools of nursing in the United States of America, and a member movement of the International Fellowship of Evangelical Students. For information about local and regional activities, write Public Relations Dept., InterVarsity Christian Fellowship, 6400 Schroeder Rd., P.O. Box 7895, Madison, WI 53707-7895.

All Scripture quotations, unless otherwise indicated, are from the Holy Bible, New International Version. Copyright © 1973, 1978, International Bible Society. Used by permission of Zondervan Bible Publishers.

Cover illustration: Tom Duckworth

ISBN 0-8308-1375-6

Printed in the United States of America ∞

Library of Congress Cataloging-in-Publication Data

Webster, Douglas D.
    Finding spiritual direction: the challenge and joys of Christian
growth/Douglas D. Webster; foreword by Eugene Peterson.
        p.   cm.
    Includes bibliographical references.
    ISBN 0-8308-1375-6
    1. Spiritual direction.   2. Bible. N.T. James—Criticism,
interpretation, etc.   I. Title.
BV5053.W43   1991
253.5'3—dc20   91-675
                                                    CIP

15	14	13	12	11	10	9	8	7	6	5	4	3	2	1
03	02	01	00	99	98	97	96	95	94	93	92	91		

For the Evangelical Community Church,
a household of faith
in Bloomington, Indiana

Foreword

There are two ways to get through the day. One is by list-making, the other by story-making. Both ways use the stuff of ordinary life, but the way they use it is very different. All lists end up looking more or less alike; every story is an original. A list-making life can be extremely useful to society, but it is the story-making life that glorifies God.

Am I going to settle into a list-making life? Is the content of my day going to consist in checking off the moral rules I have kept, the doctrinal truths I have believed, thirsty travelers to whom I have given a cup of cold water, oxen I have pulled out of the ditch? There are religious leaders who encourage this kind of behavior in us. Essentially, they are program directors who list for us what we must do and say in order to "meet the challenge" or "realize the vision"—some such euphemism or other for the program director's management takeover of the gospel. If we go down the list carefully and do exactly what we are told, we end the day with a nice sense of accomplishment. But it is the kind of accomplishment for which blue ribbons are awarded in dog shows. It is, unfortunately, the prevailing mode of religious leadership in America today.

Or am I going to insist on a story-making life? Am I going to dive into the day expectant, wondering what God in his freedom will make of my "list" of circumstances and jobs and people? We are, each of us, in the middle of a story, a God-authored story. We don't know what the next sentence is, let alone the next page. We know the plot is salvation. We know that grace is the creative energy moving it along. But we don't know what is coming next or the part we will play in it. Often we feel vulnerable and exposed. Then it dawns on us that we are being offered the immense dignity of becoming lovers and believers in this story, not told *how* to love and believe, but trusted *to* love and believe, given the *freedom* to love and believe. And in God, no less. Some days the huge mystery of this overwhelms us and we want to retreat to the tidiness of a list. On such days we are fortunate if we have access to a pastor or friend who is a spiritual director.

A spiritual director is a person who helps us use the stuff of our life in story-making, and who refuses to exploit us in list-making. There are not nearly enough of them around. There are Christians in America, their pockets and purses stuffed with lists, who have yet to meet a true spiritual director. It is the kind of religious leadership of which we are most in need, but which is least in evidence. In this book Douglas Webster helps us all, leaders and led, by going to one of the source documents of spiritual direction, the letter of James, showing us how it works, how our Lord's brother went about this necessary work and how we can go about it.

Eugene H. Peterson

Blessed are those whose strength is in you,
who have set their hearts on pilgrimage.
PSALM 84:5

1

THE
WORK
OF
SPIRITUAL
DIRECTION

L IFE as we know it lacks focus and unity. It is complex, competitive and hectic. In the face of our deepest fears and frustrations, we desperately need a coherent center that holds life together. True spiritual direction offers a lasting alternative. It provides relief from the life-squelching fragmentation of daily life in the nineties. It spares us the hassle of quick-fix, overprogrammed, simplistic solutions. It meets a genuine felt need among Christians who earnestly desire to be guided by the Word of God from immaturity to maturity, from confusion to understanding, from complexity to simplicity. True spiritual direction does not complicate life, it clarifies it.

This book aims to ease the burdens of life by focusing on spiritual direction as it is found in the book of James. I was drawn to the method and content of James's spiritual direction by my own desire to be guided by the Word of God and to offer authentic spiritual direction in pastoral ministry. This ancient yet timely piece of spiritual counsel not only gave me specific, practical direction, but also went a long way in showing me *how* a spiritual director should offer guidance. Everyone involved in spiritual leadership, from a parent to a Bible study leader to a youth pastor to a church elder, has some valuable lessons to learn from this classic example of spiritual direction. We enter into a unique relationship with this ancient prophet-pastor when we allow ourselves to be admonished and rebuked by him.

What a medical doctor does for my physical life, James does for my spiritual life. He is a physician of the soul, a brilliant diagnostician, who detects spiritual disease and accurately prescribes its remedy. From early childhood, we tend to accept the authority of doctors and to follow their advice in order to get well and stay healthy. We change our diets, take our medicine and submit to surgery. But when it comes to spiritual counsel, we feel less confident about the lines of authority. We tend to disbelieve the diagnosis and ignore the prescription. We may attempt to treat ourselves or seek the advice we want to hear rather than what we need to hear.

Spiritual authority has grown more and more difficult to recognize. What we expect of a spiritual guide may contradict the biblical model of a spiritual director. Many impressionable saints judge spiritual direction on the basis of a person's popularity, personality and cultural piety. Using these criteria, one wonders whether the apostles would be warmly received today as spiritual guides. Those who identify leadership in this way, rather than by character and wisdom, confuse spiritual counsel with personal taste and popular preference.

James does not appeal to popular taste, either in his day or in our own. That is why we have so much to gain by following his counsel. He is spiritually perceptive, practically minded and committed to Christ-centered spiritual direction. He sets us on a course of growth and maturity that goes from strength to strength and from grace to grace. Our lives, spared of simplistic solutions and trivial techniques, focus singularly on the Word of God. Maturity is measured by practical, definable commitments. And it is modeled, rather than managed or manipulated, by those who have internalized the Word of God and allowed it to shape their daily lives. True spiritual direction, as we will see in the book of James, is not a burden but a blessing. Instead of putting us down, it lifts us up. Rather than oppress, it liberates.

Simplifying Life

That spiritual direction is liberating does not necessarily pave the way for its ready acceptance by today's Christian. Established cultural patterns make it difficult to give and receive spiritual direction. Pious presumption and well-insulated comfort zones hinder the work of a spiritual director who seeks to apply the wisdom of God to the marketplace, the university and the family. The personal weaknesses and social forces which minimize Christian growth and depreciate spirituality are not only powerful but subtle. Sinful habits of the heart are not easily detected and uprooted. Weeds of self-pity and selfishness grow so fast that without serious attention they quickly destroy the "harvest of righteousness."

Many Christians have settled for the simplicity on the naive side of complexity. They do not want to be disturbed by issues that unsettle the status quo and deny them their passions and pleasures. They repeat the elementary truths of the faith over and over again, with little movement toward maturity. In the face of suffering and death, they become as vulnerable and self-centered as non-Christians, sometimes even more so. Success reinforces pride, personal opinion and independence. Failure produces resentment, insecurity and bitterness. They are "saved," but overwhelmed by waves of popular culture. Their lives follow the fashions and trends of the age. Beyond a few basic convictions, they remain as opinionated and culture-bound as the next guy. Their understanding of evil and salvation is superficial and simplistic.

The work of spiritual direction follows a very practical agenda. It helps us to distinguish the pressures and patterns that promote favoritism instead of friendship, self-indulgence instead of compassion. The ruling conformities of the world are not easily recognized, let alone transformed. They are so deeply embedded in how we think and feel that apart from true spiritual renewal, there is little hope for growth and maturity.

True spiritual directors offer a simplicity on the mature side of complexity. Rather than complicate life, they clarify it. They help us clean up the clutter of mixed motives, conflicting priorities and false values. Through the Word of God they expose the strategies of self-deception. They help us to understand the perversity and power of evil. They give serious attention to ordinary daily life as the proving ground for authentic Christian living.

Mentoring Maturity

Christian maturity is not automatic. It does not just happen by attending church or growing up in a Christian home. Christians need to be guided, nurtured and shown ways of living that are both more spiritual and more human. Perhaps the best analogy for understanding the structure of spiritual direction is parenting. Parents cannot expect to nurture and guide a child's character by passing along spiritual formulas any more than they can expect a child to remain on baby formula. Christians should reach a level of development where they prefer solid spiritual food to religious clichés and predictable sermons.

Nothing James writes is overly complicated or difficult to grasp. The meaning of his spiritual direction is relatively easy to figure out, but challenging to accept. There is a price to be paid for uncomplicating life. Clarity does not come cheap. Passage from infancy to maturity, from simplistic naiveté to mature simplicity, requires obedience and faithfulness. James does not offer ten easy steps to Christian maturity; instead, he immerses us in the spiritual struggle of life. He dishes out a full helping of solid analysis and constructive direction. He is both

SERVICE   COMMUNITY   SUBMISSION
SELF-PREOCCUPATION   ISOLATION   PRESUMPTION

prophetic and pastoral, negative and positive. He diagnoses the spiritual sickness and prescribes the biblical response. He leads us in moving our souls from self-preoccupation to service, from isolation to community, from presumption to submission. To James, spiritual direction means nothing less than growing in the grace and in the knowledge of our Lord Jesus Christ. TRUTH   THINKING

SLOGANS   BUZZ WORDS

Clarifying Guidance

If we expect James to entertain us, we will be disappointed. He is a teacher. We search in vain for amusing anecdotes. Instead, we find penetrating analysis, perceptive insight and a passion for authentic Christian living. James rebukes. He does not pacify or cajole his brothers and sisters in Christ. He does not re-evangelize believers or sermonize about suburban life. He offers guidance boldly and persuasively, as if the peace and joy of his fellow believers depends on it.

In a media-conditioned culture which has reduced communication to images and sound bites, people prefer their guidance packaged for quick and easy consumption. Weighty instruction must conform to the style of a TV commercial. Communication is abbreviated, simplified and streamlined in a creative but futile quest to deliver a message with a punch. So much of today's effort lies in reducing great truths, which deserve careful reflection and analysis, to memorable slogans. If we are not careful, buzzwords may replace thinking.

James communicates directly, person-to-person, without distracting gimmicks and ploys. He never hesitates to level with his readers, nor to impress upon them the gravity of their situation. He assumes the task of training in righteousness with intensity. We might prefer our spiritual director to be easygoing and laid back. But James is the kind of spiritual director we need.

James weans us away from a fast-food spiritual diet. He doesn't cater to "drive-thru" spirituality or microwavable truth. Instead of compromising our spiritual diet to fit our lifestyle, he nourishes our lifestyle with a proper spiritual diet. He does not handle the Word of

God cleverly, but faithfully. He has no desire to impress people with his ingenuity or his sense of humor. James simply wants to cause people to think long and hard about the integrity of their commitment to Christ. The seriousness of our own spiritual condition, as well as that of the church, commends James's simple, direct approach. Life is no laughing matter. In this age of fragmentation, when we feel so confused and out of focus, we need a brother in Christ who will not humor us but guide us. In James we have such a brother.

James deals with issues as they come to us in life—not in a neatly organized, A-to-Z fashion, but in the rough and tumble of everyday living. Spirituality is not cut off from practicality. It belongs in the middle of daily life with its trials, tensions and tedium. It is as close to us as the words in our mouth and the feelings of our heart. It is concerned with ambition and anxiety, suffering and success, insecurity and self-confidence. Those who wish to ignore troublesome issues will quickly lose interest in James. But those who want a handle on dealing with suffering, disappointment and empty piety will find James to be a valuable spiritual guide.

True spiritual direction not only challenges; it comforts. It lifts from our shoulders the burden of unobtainable goals, false hopes and unreasonable expectations. Lives are set free from wrong-headed activism and self-righteous crusades. True spiritual directors, like James, attack spiritual presumption in all its forms. Instead of puffing up our ego and stimulating emotional highs, they nurture a steadfast resolve to live for God. If we follow their example, we leave behind the hype of a religious circus and participate in biblical community, helping people turn away from sin and toward God in Christ. True spirituality transforms ordinary living into an extraordinary witness to the grace and peace of Jesus Christ. I commend to you the work of James as a model of spiritual direction. I encourage you to follow his example and learn by heart the style, substance and structure of his spiritual direction. With James as our guide, we will not only deepen our commitment to Jesus Christ, but learn to assist others in moving from immaturity to maturity.

This offering of spiritual direction issues directly from the challenge and the comfort of a body of believers in Bloomington, Indiana. Without their on-the-job training in the ancient and timely art of spiritual direction, I would never have written this book. I am grateful to these fellow travelers who have shared in the journey beyond felt needs. Their faithfulness in Christ has made the long obedience in the same direction the only route worth taking.

Through the joy and pain of pastoral ministry I have, in Ginny, the best companion possible. Her love and honesty work their own spiritual direction in my life. With Jeremy, Andrew and Kennerly, our spiritual pilgrimage is not only a challenge, but a great joy.

Rodney Clapp, the editor I worked with at InterVarsity Press, has been sensitive throughout to the shape and tone of this spiritual direction. His advice and encouragement are much appreciated.

FAITHFULLY
CLEVERLY

2

FROM
PUBLIC
RELATIONS
TO
SPIRITUAL
DIRECTION

I WOULD like to meet James someday. His straightforward manner reminds me of my father. I grew up impressed with my father's no-nonsense approach to life. He adopted the stark work ethic of his immigrant parents, devoid of trivialities and indulgences. He had no interest in small talk or petty concerns.

When my high-school friends ridiculed their fathers and joked about deceiving the "old man," I knew I had a unique dad. It never even occurred to me to go against him, not because I dreaded his punishment, but because I had complete confidence in him. I was under his authority, right where I belonged. Rarely did it seem like a burden. Even when we disagreed or I disobeyed, the relationship of love and respect persisted. A math teacher by profession, but a carpenter by avocation, he nailed convictions as precisely as he drove a nail into a two-by-four. He hated hypocrisy and loved honesty. His spirituality was concrete and practical. He shied away from those who spiritualized reality, whose piety seemed more show than substance. My father's character stands out in a day when many men are self-absorbed wimps who, having lost confidence in their convictions, waffle between sentiment and distraction. When I read James, I think of the down-to-earth spiritual direction I grew up on.

There is a strength and definiteness about James's approach to spirituality that I wish to emulate. He is concise in his communication, passionate about the truth and compassionate toward those in need. He has no tolerance for evil and denounces disobedience without a hint of self-righteousness. He is neither ego-driven nor self-promoting. James reveals his servant heart by losing himself in the task of spiritual direction. He is a prophet and a pastor, immersed in the struggle for obedience. I find the depth and character of his spiritual direction impressive and the vigor of his writing both convicting and reassuring.

Today's church needs more pastors like James. We have plenty of personnel to run our programs and promote goodwill, but we have few spiritual directors who will level with us the way James does. Though the vocation of prophet-pastor is a viable one, I have never seen a job description for one or read the title "John Smith, Prophet-Pastor" on the back of a church bulletin. It doesn't surprise me that such people should be in short supply. Who, after all, relishes bucking the pious expectations and triviality of the Bible Belt? Serving as a protagonist of God's will has its drawbacks, especially when the people of God seem to need one.

If a prophet-pastor of the caliber of James were around today, he would not speak about what to us is controversial; he would probably address what we have come to accept as normal and commonplace. We would find ourselves amused or frustrated because he would seem to be making a great fuss about nothing at all. At least that is how we might see it. He would concentrate on the inconsistencies, misconceptions and hypocrisies of counterfeit Christianity.

A prophet like James would oppose all forms of spiritual presumption. He would be preeminently practical and specific in his counsel. Those accustomed to vague generalities might find his spiritual direction too direct, but many others would find his counsel refreshing and helpful. People expecting a pastor to ask, "What do you think?" or "How do you feel about that?" might find the prophet-pastor's penetrating truthfulness meddling, his perspective patronizing and his rhetoric haranguing.

The common mores of church life, such as the outward show of religion, preoccupation with personal opinion, concentration on self-interest, depreciation of the poor, frequency of gossip, efforts to "succeed," a self-indulgent lifestyle and the appearance of faith all pose a great challenge to authentic Christianity. But this challenge goes largely unnoticed. It has become routine and commonplace.

Precisely when the people of God are comfortable with their moral decorum and pious atmosphere, the Lord calls in the prophet-pastor. Some feel he boldly proclaims God's Word, but most think he is making too much of small indiscretions and well-intentioned habits.

Can you imagine the reaction if a prophet like James were called to a church in America's heartland? How would he be received in a church that measures success by the number of "giving units," and equates Christianity with being nice? I am afraid that wherever the body of Christ has degenerated into a collection of consumers, clients and spectators, wherever congregational opinion has prevailed, and wherever style has won over spirituality, a prophet-pastor would be unwelcome.

Terms of Endearment

The way people evaluate pastors today reflects the spirit of the times more than the Spirit of Christ. In our narcissistic culture, if a pastor wants to impress people, he has to convince them that he exists solely for them. His job is to meet their expectations, that is, the expectations of a self-centered, consumer-oriented society that believes the customer is always right. There is, however, a great difference between customer service and Christian service. Under society's terms of endearment, people are given what they want, not what they need. In exchange for services rendered, spiritual leaders receive applause and power. Ministry is reviewed by the audience as a performance, rather than received by the body of Christ as spiritual direction.

James resists the sentiment that it is more important for pastors to be likeable than to be holy. He would challenge the notion that the pastor's personality is more crucial to congregational acceptance than his Christian character or discernment. James is a New Testament Jeremiah burdened with the task of spiritual direction. His single-minded intensity and passion for Christ might make him seem unapproachable, even formidable, especially to those who want their pastor to be "huggable" and "vulnerable." If James were around today, some well-intentioned church elder might advise him to lighten up and quit taking life so seriously.

Under these terms of endearment, the public-relations pastor knows that the moment of exchange at the back of the sanctuary is more important than hours of prayer and study. Better to master the art of small talk than cultivate the disciplines of the Spirit. Better to feign interest in trivial details of a parishioner's life than to pray the Psalms. Pastoral success depends on making people feel important, communicating humorously, pulling on people's heartstrings, motivating them to contribute to the church. Witty self-expression is more important than personal self-control. A generation attracted to preachers who go for the tears instead of the brain may reduce Christianity to personal testimonies without theology and Christian living without ethics.

If James were alive today, I believe he would warn that our terms of endearment, for all their popularity and appeal, are producing counterfeit Christians. The misguided energy of the church creates a false spiritual atmosphere. We want to be known as a friendly church, but we know little about friendship. We want a warm, outgoing pastor and well-run programs for all ages, but we know little about being holy and using our spiritual gifts. We want fellowship, but we do not know how to relate to one another through the Word of God, prayer and worship. The common bond in Christ is more rhetorical than real, a cliché rather than a commitment. If there ever was a time we needed the counsel of James, it is now. We need his depth, his passion, his intense concern for authentic Christianity.

Not too long ago a woman shared with me the reason for her eighteen-year-old daughter's rejection of Christianity. Painfully she described their conversations. Her daughter claimed that she could have nothing to do with Christ because of the superficiality of her mother. Her mother had no depth. Her life was trivial, her faith sentimental, her interests frivolous. Their conversations rarely went beyond small talk. She held her mother responsible for a conspiracy of silence on a host of issues she was now confronting head-on at college. She might as well have walked on campus from the desert as from middle-class suburbia.

Her mother sobbed and blurted out, "My daughter is right! I am superficial. I am still a child. I was raised in a church that only thought about numbers and slogans, and I've never gone beyond that. For all these years I've never grown up, never thought about what is important." As I listened to her, I marveled at her honesty and thanked God for the work of the Holy Spirit in helping her realize her need to grow. It would have been wrong to deny her superficiality. Her confession and repentance before God were necessary. The honesty and openness she is now having with her daughter signals hope for both of them. The book of James confronts our commonplace superficiality and encourages us to reexamine the meaning of authentic Christianity.

Humility and Authority
In America's marketplace of pious moods and religious excitement, the apostle Paul's words suffer terrible abuse: "I have become all things to all men so that by all possible means I might save some" (1 Cor 9:22).

In light of today's casual spirituality based on cultural conformity, what does Paul mean? Should we become trite to save the frivolous, materialistic to save the greedy, or sexy to save the promiscuous? Are we so shaped by culture that we have little heart for honest, no-nonsense spiritual direction? James guides us into what it means to be a spiritual director. He shows what it really means to become all things to all people for the sake of Christ. In James we have a true spiritual mentor who cares little about what people think of him and much about their spiritual growth and well-being.

James describes himself very briefly as "a servant of God and of the Lord Jesus Christ." A long-standing tradition attributes the letter to James, the brother of Jesus, the same James who possibly presided over the Jerusalem council (Acts 15) and who was described by the apostle Paul as a pillar of the church (Gal 2:9). He does not argue for his spiritual authority, he assumes it. From the outset James implies that the humility of Christ's slave is consistent with the authority of a strong spiritual director. Today we tend to separate humility and authority as incompatible. James did not. His humility and authority were inseparable.

Unfortunately, humility is no longer defined biblically but emotively. It is a matter of personality more than an attribute of character and a work of grace. From God's perspective, humility is obedience to his Word. It is a virtue received and nurtured by grace. It involves submitting our minds and lives to the lordship of Jesus Christ. Humility is the moment-by-moment, act-of-the-will decision to center life on Christ rather than self. There is no room for self-salvation and foolish pride. We are saved by grace and not by works, lest anyone should boast.

Jesus illustrates the profound relationship between self-worth and self-sacrifice. Humble service and spiritual authority go together. We are told that before Jesus began to wash the disciples' feet, he "*knew* that the Father had put all things under his power, and that he had come from God and was returning to God" (Jn 13:3). Humility and authority are not mutually exclusive. They are, in fact, inseparable. By his up-front assertion that he is "a servant of God and of the Lord Jesus Christ," it is clear James knows that his authority depends upon his humility. He is qualified to give spiritual direction as long as he humbly submits to the Word of God.

"What we suffer from today," G. K. Chesterton wrote, "is humility in the wrong place." Humility has moved from ambition to conviction. "A man was meant to be doubtful about himself, but undoubting about the truth; this has been exactly reversed. Nowadays the part of a man that a man does assert is exactly the part he ought not to assert—himself. The part he doubts is exactly the part he ought not to doubt—the Divine Reason."[1]

Spiritual authority is the natural corollary to Christlike humility. People who truly submit to God reflect discernment and wisdom. Their counsel is accepted or rejected precisely because they represent the will of God. James sees no inconsistency in claiming to be a slave of Christ and speaking powerfully on behalf of God.

James is authoritative but not authoritarian. He reasons with his fellow believers: "Consider it pure joy . . ."; "My dear brothers, take note of this . . ."; "Listen, my dear brothers . . ." James cannot force them to follow God's way, but he does challenge, encourage, exhort and entreat.

One important way spiritual directors love those they minister to is by refusing to make a big deal about themselves. We suffer a polite perversity today that James would disapprove of. We put our leaders on a pedestal in an odd sort of way. We used to idealize the "giants" of the faith, great missionaries and preachers, who achieved more for God than we could ever dream of accomplishing. Our lives and faith seemed puny next to these heroes of the faith. Their biographies made them larger than life and canonized their efforts. They were truly in a class by themselves, their spirituality measured in manly feats of faith reverently retold by loyal followers. They pumped excitement into the faith and gave people something to idealize. Their oil portraits adorn the walls of Christian institutions and their biographies continue to be read.

Although we still go in for "giants" of the faith, especially converted sports stars and rich entrepreneurs with a personal testimony, today's pedestal is occupied by spiritual leaders who are transparent, self-revealing, and vulnerable. We do not idealize their spiritual experience as much as we empathize with it. Their lives become the human-interest story surrounding the good news. They personalize the faith by experiencing a range of emotions for us. We do not want a hero of the faith commanding attention; we want a fellow-struggler telling us how it feels. We want them to be weak as we are weak. In the Sunday morning sermon we want to hear an adult version of spiritual Show and Tell. This relieves our boredom with the faith and reassures us that we are human. It helps us to rationalize our own spiritual weakness. After all, if the pastor struggles with all the things we are struggling with, then we don't feel so bad. We picture the pastor on the pedestal—but only in order to be spiritually naked.

Recently I heard a pastor preaching on the subject of personality. He contrasted what he described as the apostle Paul's hard-driving, task-oriented temperament with his own more laid-back, easygoing disposition. You could almost feel the relief spreading through the audience, as if he had just assured them it was okay to be casual about their faith. They laughed when he said, "You know, I don't think Paul and I would get along very well." When he said that, he instantly endeared himself to all those who didn't think they could get along with Paul either. His gratuitous self-expression translated into something like this: "It's okay to hang loose. I'm an easygoing guy and I like people who go with the flow." He may not have intended to communicate this; perhaps he thought that the contrast between himself and Paul would make the message more interesting and get a laugh. But this is part of the problem: pastors care more about saying something cute than communicating truth. I wondered whether he would have said the same thing if Paul were sitting in the front row.

What many want in a pastor is not a teacher or a mentor, but a spiritual celebrity through whom they vicariously live out the Christian life. It is not unlike the habit in some cultures of paying mourners to wail over a deceased relative. Similarly, many of us want to pay a pastor to be on call around the clock to meet felt needs. Between emotional crises, we live independently of spiritual counsel: Who needs a doctor when we are feeling good? But as soon as an emotional demand arises, we expect the pastor to spring into action, just like the family doctor who makes house calls. We want the pastor to care if we are having our foot operated on, or if we are struggling in our marriage, or if our distant cousin is dying of cancer. And certainly a pastor *should* care about what is happening in our lives. But I am suggesting that we have substituted this form of felt-need-oriented care for spiritual direction. We would prefer to pay someone to listen to our complaints and laments than to hear someone speak the word of God into our brokenness and pain.

We have lost the distinction between felt needs and spiritual needs. Felt needs center on my immediate emotional wants. I want to feel consoled or loved or excited. Spiritual needs center on God and my understanding of his will in my total life situation. Under society's terms of endearment pastors do not equip the laity for works of service. They entertain, manage and role-play for the collective religious experience of the congregation. James is not a modern pastor, selling himself and the gospel to a religious consumer. On the contrary, James addresses specific, discernable spiritual needs out of the Word of God and the integrity of his own commitment to Christ.

In Christian love James does not pander to the modern appetite for anecdotal tidbits. He refuses to confuse spiritual needs with self-centered felt needs. He rejects the temptation to intersperse forceful spiritual insight and direction with cute stories of suburban drama, sports highlights, and what he did on his day off.

Negative Capability
We cannot dismiss the example of James because he wrote in another

era. Both the content of his message and the manner of his communication are instructive for the church today and guided by the Spirit of God. James does not turn the responsibility of spiritual direction into an opportunity for self-expression. He draws attention to the Word of God, not to himself. James has no intention of establishing his own school of thought or setting out a distinctive version of spirituality. Instead of publicizing himself in pastoral ministry he loses himself.

Good actors and actresses know how to play a part so their own distinctive personalities are hidden. They play the part well by losing themselves in the characters. I am not suggesting James is an actor, nor am I saying that his personality is hidden. Actually a great deal of his temperament comes through his writing, as it does with all good writers. But I am saying that James submits himself in every way to a higher purpose than displaying himself. It would be highly inappropriate for a minister at a wedding ceremony to say and do things to draw attention to himself. And who could tolerate a minister or elder who used the celebration of the Lord's table to tell homey stories or funny anecdotes?

What does come through in every line of James's letter is his passionate desire that his brothers and sisters in Christ be found faithful and obedient. He is writing to a community of believers, not a collection of individualists. He addresses the church as a body of believers, a brotherhood, the household of faith. He does not want anyone to wander from the truth. To that end he is vigilant, perceptive and determined. With a prophet-pastor like James offering us spiritual direction, we have much to gain by heeding his Spirit-inspired wisdom.

Consider it pure joy, my brothers, whenever you face
trials of many kinds, because you know that the testing
of your faith develops perseverance. Perseverance must
finish its work so that you may be mature and
complete, not lacking anything. If any of you lacks
wisdom, he should ask God, who gives generously to all
without finding fault, and it will be given to him. But
when he asks, he must believe and not doubt, because
he who doubts is like a wave of the sea, blown and
tossed by the wind. That man should not think he will
receive anything from the Lord; he is a double-minded
man, unstable in all he does.

JAMES 1:2-8

3

FROM
FALSE
EXPECTATIONS
TO
PEACE
AND JOY

IMAGINE that the notoriety of Martin Luther's dismissal of James as "an epistle of straw" can be credited to the popular feeling that there is something not quite right about James. Luther felt that the book of James emphasized the law instead of promoting Christ. As a result, Luther gave James a "second-class" status in the canon of Scripture and a disparaging reputation that has been hard to shake. What concerned Luther, and still bothers many Christians today, is that James does not fit their expectation of gospel preaching.

Effective Evangelism
Nor does James fit many Christians' definition of evangelism. There is no mention of the cross or the resurrection. Justification by faith is not

developed as in Paul's epistles. And the name Jesus Christ appears only twice—first, to identify the object of James's service, and second, to recognize the one in whom he and his readers believed. Those who look for the repetition of certain biblical themes may be unsettled by James.

I have heard preachers say that a sermon is not a sermon unless people are told how to be saved. Many Americans define preaching as a call to the unbeliever to receive Christ. Sunday after Sunday they offer their congregation a recital of the "plan of salvation." They preach the elementary teachings about Christ over and over again. After years of predictable sermons, the congregation comes to believe that anything more elaborate smacks of intellectualizing the gospel. Young people and adults gain little idea of the Bible's practical relevance to their daily responsibilities and relationships. Those who need the reassurance of Christian clichés may have trouble adjusting to James. The brother of our Lord does not preach the way many are used to. He never once speaks of being "born again" or of the need for a "personal relationship with Jesus." He refuses to be either elementary or repetitive. Since he intended his letter for a Christian readership, he wastes no time convincing Christians of what they already know. He simply assumes their understanding of the historical Jesus, his sacrificial death and glorious resurrection. And he goes on from there to explore positive patterns of Christlike behavior that will have true evangelistic impact.

Contrary to popular opinion, James presents one of the best forms of evangelistic preaching possible. What could be more convincing than for the unsaved person to see Christians forsake their common sins and obey a serious call to authentic Christian living? The evangelism of James is very practical. Take down the façade of false spirituality and see the positive effect on our neighbors. Remove the trappings of showy religious piety and relieve our colleagues. Back up our talk with compassion and justice and maybe people will listen to the gospel. Expose the compromise with evil and gain the attention of our children. Forsake the world's wisdom. End favoritism. Love the widow and then maybe the gospel will be good news to those around us. Wherever the word of truth shapes believers' lives, wc will find true evangelism. James may not have spoken of the cross as such, but everything he says points to it and flows from it. The preaching of James centers on the demanding task of internalizing one's faith. From beginning to end, it is obvious that James has been with Jesus.

Misleading Expectations

Corresponding with sojourners who are "scattered among the nations," living in a world they cannot call home, James wastes no time getting down to spiritual direction. In a few short lines he handles one of the most popular misconceptions facing Christians today. It is summed up in a convenience store ad which proudly proclaims, "Where the Good Things Come Easy!" From material success to intimate sex, from academic achievement to getting in shape, we want the shortest and quickest route to the top. This philosophy is stamped all over our culture.

We have become so accustomed to the immediate availability of consumer goods that we also expect to possess traits such as perseverance and wisdom on demand. But that is not how spiritual maturity works. The methods of acquiring material goods do not help us in shaping character. In fact, they make it more difficult. For many, life has never been easier: ample leisure time, financial security, gourmet diets, health club work-outs and beautiful homes. But the flip side of that lifestyle exposes hectic schedules, shallow relationships, scattered lives, addiction patterns and a nagging conclusion that life is meaningless. While it is a class act on the outside, it seems like slave labor on the inside.

If James found it necessary to remind first-century believers that "trials of many kinds" were instrumental in cultivating maturity, how much more do we need that emphasis today. We are so tempted to carry the consumer mentality right into the center of our lives and allow it to shape all our expectations. We want easy access to spiritual maturity, but there is no software for programming perseverance. We want an easy familiarity with the things of God, yet fail to recognize that the whole counsel of God requires years of reflection and internalizing.

Many have been given a false impression that accepting Christ will make life easier. Suffering will be reduced, trials overcome and God's wonderful plan will commence. James does not agree with this ad campaign of pop Christianity. Instead, he tells us to resist thinking that the difficulties of life that help develop character and depth will be eliminated. James is clear and unambiguous. His perspective is both challenging and reassuring. The Christian life is not where the good things come easy. Pure joy is found in a life of growth, not in a life of ease.

We may know this and find ourselves agreeing with James, but find it difficult to accept and apply. It is both humbling and encouraging for me to observe the growth of a young Christian couple I've known for years. Pete and Julie have five children. Three are healthy, normal kids, but two have significant physical disabilities.

Timmy, their second child, was born legally blind. You can imagine how tough this was on a young couple. Normal hopes and expectations were suddenly exchanged for a difficult set of problems. Pete's dreams of fishing with his son gave way to seemingly unsurmountable concerns. By the time their fourth child was born, Pete and Julie had acclimated well to Timmy's disability. They had gone beyond coping to thriving. Their family was happier and stronger because of Timmy's challenge. But then Marybeth was born with Down's syndrome. Once again their hopes and dreams for their precious newborn were suddenly dashed. She too would never be able to live a "normal" life. Like Timmy, she posed a special challenge to her parents, demanding extra time, energy and resources. But today Pete and Julie rejoice in Marybeth, a little girl whose love permeates the family in a way no one else's could. The challenge of parenting children such as Timmy and Beth—along with three other kids—seems overwhelming to many of us. But Pete and Julie have learned to do much more than cope. Their family life is a witness to God's love in action. Trials have not disabled them but strengthened them. Friends are not aware of their loss as much as of their love. When they speak of God's sovereign care, they make it easier for others to trust in God. Their lives reflect the peace and joy of a persevering faith.

Passionate Counsel

The way someone communicates to us is very important. We probably pick up the tone of voice and body language faster than the content of what is said. A person's tone of voice may convey regard or disregard for us. A cutting or sarcastic edge puts us on the defensive. A comforting, reassuring tone makes us more receptive to the message. If something is said casually or indifferently, we are more inclined to dismiss it as unimportant. If on the other hand something comes across with passion and intensity, we know that the speaker finds the content important. As I read through the book of James, I sometimes wish I had a tape recording of his voice so I could hear the tone he used. Instead, we have to look for other clues to pick up his tone. James knew that there was more to tone than voice inflection. In just a few short verses (1:2-8) he uses a number of pointers to indicate the tone of his spiritual direction. The first verb is an imperative—"*Consider* it pure joy"—showing us that he is appealing to the readers' will. He is not simply stating a fact. He is entreating, imploring, beseeching them to receive the truth he is expressing. By using the imperative, he assumes a place of authority in giving them counsel. He is completely convinced of the reliability of his words, yet there is no hint of superiority in his tone. His authority comes across with deep affinity for those he refers to as "my brothers." Like an older brother who genuinely cares, he speaks with both emphasis and empathy.

In his appeal for readers to accept God's perspective, James reveals an underlying respect for their insight and comprehension. His spiritual direction rests on an important assumption—expressed sincerely, not patronizingly: "Consider it pure joy . . . *because you know* that the testing of your faith develops perseverance." He is building on what they already know, reminding them thoughtfully and passionately that they need to take this truth to heart.

His choice of words conveys a special intensity and concern. There is a big difference between saying, "I hope you will agree with me that trials can be a good thing," and declaring, "Consider it pure joy, my brothers, whenever you face trials of many kinds." There is an exceptional quality to this joy; it is "pure joy." And the trials are broadly inclusive, personally encountered and experienced at any time.

James draws out the character-developing benefit of suffering by repeating the strong word "perseverance" twice and affirming the goal of becoming "mature and complete, not lacking anything." He emphatically underscores the positive advantage of growing through all kinds of difficulties. His counsel exudes strength and confidence in God. There is absolutely no question in James's mind of God's sufficiency to meet the needs of those who turn to God for wisdom. He boldly affirms, "it will be given to him."

The intensity continues in James's description of the person who does not look to God amid trials. Such a person is as chaotic and confused as the churning sea. Just as his earlier imperative "Consider it pure joy" is not a suggestion but a heartfelt command, James's pronouncement here is not a mild caution but a grave warning. The great benefits of spiritual growth through adversity are matched by a dire admonition to the one who refuses to turn to God for help: "That one should not think he will receive anything from the Lord; he is a double-minded person, unstable in all he does" (vv. 7-8).

We should read James's words with the force and concern that he intended. His tone was authoritative, compassionate and convincing. He did not hold these views lightly. Nor did he express them without regard for the believers he earnestly sought to help. With passion but not anger, he offered vital spiritual direction, the kind we need to hear today if we are to know the peace and joy of Christ.

Instead of devising ways to escape our suffering, we need to grow through our suffering. This past year several people came to me seeking counsel about their involvement in homosexual relationships. Each one expressed the conviction that what they were doing was wrong. They were convinced on biblical grounds and personal experience that homosexual practice was sinful and violated their relationship with Christ. They needed no direction from me in defining the sin. What they needed was what they came for: encouragement and support to end sexual relationships that were wrong. If I had compromised biblical truth by denying the sinfulness of homosexual practice, I would have been as guilty as if I had committed the sin myself. But if I had made light of the personal suffering and emotional pain involved in breaking off homosexual relationships, I would have also proved to be a deceptive spiritual director. To resist a deeply instilled—though misguided—sexual drive is a very painful test of faith. Brothers and sisters in Christ experiencing this ordeal need our loving empathy and support if they are to persevere. They need spiritual directors who will neither deny their sin nor ignore the pain involved in overcoming it. Together we need to affirm that there is no shortcut around the suffering, but that through the suffering God's grace will be sufficient for our weakness.

Prayer

At the heart of James's spiritual direction is a fresh reminder of our dependence upon God for wisdom. The purpose of spiritual direction is not to fashion a substitute for God but to point people to God. Good counsel leads people to center their thoughts and lives on God. "If any of you lacks wisdom" (and who doesn't?), "he should ask of God, who gives generously to all without finding fault, and it will be given to him" (v. 5). People who do not worship and pray lack the stability and security to live in a world of upheaval. They are tossed around by every wind of adversity and wave of suffering. They live on a flood plain, oblivious to their vulnerability and ignorant of the dangers. They balk at the prospect of moving to higher ground. They like it too much where they are. Instead of cultivating the maturity to turn to God for the wisdom that sees all of life as serving his purposes, we fend for ourselves. Schools, hospitals, counseling centers, even churches divert us from attending to God. We no longer pray for wisdom, we pay for advice. We buy clothes for self-confidence and insurance for security. In a busy world of hyperactivity, prayer seems dysfunctional, unproductive, a waste of time. We ought to be out there doing something. But it all amounts to chasing the wind.

Prayer sustains the resistance of the soul against a dangerous undertow of evil. Without God, no matter how much money and status I may possess, I am lost at sea and in desperate need of rescue. The wisdom required to live in the world cannot be bought, earned or invented. The wisdom of God is given by God and must be asked for. This does not mean that when we pray everything will be placed in order and we'll feel great. Prayer does not tidy up life and arrange it in labeled file folders.[1] It focuses and intensifies life. Prayer orients our thinking, directs our actions and prepares us for God's work. Through prayer I am brought face to face with my Creator. Prayer centers my life in the will and work of the living God. Instead of grabbing, clutching and scratching, I receive God's understanding of how to live in a world unlivable without him.

God is not stingy, dispensing grace begrudgingly and wisdom piecemeal. God "gives sincerely, without hesitation or mental reservation. He does not grumble or criticize."[2] His commitment to all those who call on his name is total and unreserved. James is emphatic: If we turn to God we will not be disappointed.

When my father was dying of cancer, I grew very tired of praying yet continued to do so. There were no other satisfying options. But after describing my father's condition and praying for doctors over and over again, I found nothing to say. I sat in silence. My whole prayer consisted of "Lord . . . Lord . . ." Everything else seemed superfluous. I had run out of words. At that point the apostle Paul's promise in

Romans 8:26 took on new meaning for me: "The Spirit helps us in our weakness. We do not know what we ought to pray for, but the Spirit himself intercedes for us with groans that words cannot express." Through prayer I received the strength and comfort I needed to rest in the promise of Jesus: "I am the resurrection and the life. He who believes in me will live, even though he dies" (Jn 11:25).

People who refuse the help of God are perpetual takers, spiritual addicts who sap the strength of others because they are unwilling to turn to God for wisdom. Without God's wisdom they see no need to share their possessions, support the needy and correct those who are going astray. They indulge themselves in their own opinions and preferences. They require sermonic spoon-feeding and religious baby-sitting. Since they have rejected the wisdom of God, there is very little their brothers and sisters in Christ can do for them but observe their instability, inconsistency and double-mindedness. There is a high price, James warns, for refusing to turn to God in the midst of the struggle.

Applied Wisdom

Is there anyone who doesn't need this practical counsel? If you are like me, you probably find it easy to forget that "My help comes from the Lord, the Maker of heaven and earth" (Ps 121:2). The false impression that life ought to be trouble free and blessed with success is deeply ingrained within us. Far from calculating the positive effects of growth through trials, I find myself figuring out every possible way to avoid difficulties. No doubt we feel freer to dispense James's advice than to receive it.

We all know believers who love to quote Bible verses and tell people how to feel and what to do. They show little compassion or empathy, but take great pride in having all the right answers. They tend to lift good counsel out of the context of meaningful spiritual direction and drive it home from a distance. Hurting people get the distinct impression that well-meaning, proof-texting "comforters" of this sort are secretly glad not to be in their shoes. The fact is, we will always have plenty of "Job's counselors" waiting in the wings, ready to play God. But that does not mean we should avoid the direct counsel of James or be turned off by his practical, Spirit-led wisdom.

I remember an occasion when I especially needed James's applied wisdom in my life. After months of criticism and "power-plays" in my church, I felt like escaping as far as I could from pastoral ministry. The pressure seemed unrelenting and was taking its toll. I had never experienced such hate and animosity, much of it directed toward me personally. To gain some perspective, my wife, Ginny, and I traveled to Baltimore one weekend to visit Eugene and Jan Peterson. I had been so impressed and helped by Peterson's perspective on pastoral ministry that I had called him to asked if we could meet together over dinner. It seemed like an act of desperation, traveling from Indiana to Maryland to meet someone I had never talked with before. I was groping and I needed help. I felt the Lord was leading us to make this important visit.

The Petersons received us warmly and listened to our sharing. We began in Eugene's study and ended six hours later at a restaurant. They listened, asked questions, shared a few experiences of their own and offered encouragement. Neither Eugene nor Jan were quick to say what we should do, but they helped us understand the meaning of what we were going through. We left feeling reaffirmed, knowing that the ugly opposition at church did not mean we were displeasing to God or that our ministry was a failure. Their simple counsel—that good work often takes place in the midst of struggle—reassured us.

A few days after our visit I received a letter from Eugene. He wrote:
On Saturday morning, after our Friday evening conversation, I was praying the Psalms. I began at Psalm 37 and went through 40. Each one, in different ways, seemed to pick up an aspect of our conversation and put it before the Lord.

And so, as I have continued to think and pray I want to urge you to not be too eager to solve the problems and get rid of the suffering that is coming from a murmuring congregation. And to believe that

God knew what kind of congregation that was when he called you there—that perhaps the pain they inflict is being used to the purposes of holiness in you.

Among the early church fathers there was a saying to the effect, "The best bishop is a bad bishop." Meaning: The purpose, spiritually, of a bishop is that pastors learn obedience; if the bishop always gives reasonable and just commands, it is easy to obey, but if unreasonable and unjust then we *really* learn obedience and humility. Substitute "congregation" for "bishop" and we are in a strenuous school in vocational holiness.

This is nothing new to you, I know. But then nothing true is! I know you get worn down by the criticisms and misunderstandings—but I was struck very forcibly about how Davidic and psalmic your present experience is.

The peace of the Lord,
Eugene

I still struggle over Eugene's advice, but I know it is true and that James would certainly agree with it. I find it very difficult to "consider it pure joy." I don't like trials, any trials, let alone the wild assortment the world manages to dish out. The impulse to escape is strong. The temptation to meet evil with evil is constant. At times I vacillate between anger and despair. But the counsel of James, Eugene and any other true spiritual director focuses on the spiritual benefit of the struggle. I believe it is worth it to be enrolled in "a strenuous school in vocational holiness."

Those who sow in tears
will reap with songs of joy.
He who goes out weeping,
carrying seed to sow,
will return with songs of joy,
carrying sheaves with him. (Ps 126:5-6)

The brother in humble circumstances ought to take pride in his high position. But the one who is rich should take pride in his low position, because he will pass away like a wild flower. For the sun rises with scorching heat and withers the plant; its blossom falls and its beauty is destroyed. In the same way, the rich man will fade away even while he goes about his business.

Blessed is the man who perseveres under trial, because when he has stood the test, he will receive the crown of life that God has promised to those who love him.

When tempted, no one should say, "God is tempting me." For God cannot be tempted by evil, nor does he tempt anyone; but each one is tempted when, by his own evil desire, he is dragged away and enticed. Then, after desire has conceived, it gives birth to sin; and sin, when it is full-grown, gives birth to death.

Don't be deceived, my dear brothers. Every good and perfect gift is from above, coming down from the Father of the heavenly lights, who does not change like shifting shadows. He chose to give us birth through the word of truth, that we might be a kind of firstfruits of all he created.

JAMES 1:9-18

4
FROM
SELF-PITY
TO
HUMILITY

T HE prophet-pastor zeroes in on those who take a double-minded approach to life. If we are not careful, we may find ourselves caught between two worlds. As the Chinese would say, we are trying to balance with "a foot in two boats." We vacillate between the mind of Christ and the mindset of the world. We acknowledge the wisdom of our spiritual director: trials shape Christian character. Wisdom is found in God. Stability and consistency belong to those who obey God. But the value system of the world has permeated every pore and seeped into our bloodstream. Success and pleasure seem far more important than easily quoted spiritual maxims. We are tempted to spiritualize our worldly desires.

James challenges the world's value system on two fronts. We must not assume that the path to spiritual maturity is paved with success.

Nor should we allow our self-esteem to be shaped by circumstances. If we are torn between a Christian understanding of maturity and self-esteem and the world's view of success and status, we are setting ourselves up for disillusionment. A double-minded approach to life invariably ends up disappointed with God. We feel like the Lord is setting us up and withholding his best. He hasn't made good on his promises. We presume that God works to our advantage in a manner that the world will recognize. But that is not God's promise, nor is it the perspective of our spiritual director.

Humble Circumstances

James wrote to Christians who for the most part were poor. They struggled economically in a marketplace that was anything but impressed with their commitment to Christ. Many were discriminated against because they joined the Christian community. In their humble circumstances it was easy to feel impoverished and humiliated. They naturally assumed the mindset of the world and lowered their self-esteem accordingly.

Surrounded by media images of sexual perfection and material prosperity, we too can feel physically and socially inferior. Today's consumer culture sells an image of self-worth that is skin deep and paper thin. The people portrayed for our envy and emulation are products of elaborate staging and marketing strategies. Sex appeal and money buy self-worth in this culture. This is true among Christians as well. Our slick promotional publications often highlight the beautiful and successful believers. Christians plagiarize the world and project an image that despises humble circumstances. No doubt James would have great difficulty with the approach we have generally chosen to depict the Christian ideal.

Humble circumstances are difficult to escape. Most Christians I know live in humble situations. Their jobs are mundane, their looks average. They don't feel very successful or look very photogenic. When they walk through the mall no one looks twice. They get by on their incomes, but money is tight. They are not poor in any sense that James would have judged material poverty. They are certainly not poor compared to the rest of the world where vast numbers of people have no food or shelter. But they worry about car payments, tuition fees and health-care bills. This kind of "humility" is not a passing phase that they are going through. It will dog them for the rest of their earthly lives. They will always feel the humility of lackluster looks, scarce resources and frustrating relationships.

When James said, "The brother in humble circumstances ought to take pride in his high position," he was not condoning mediocrity or excusing sloth. He was simply facing the reality of humble circumstances. He was sparing Christians from living under an illusion. Today we call that illusion the American Dream—the belief that people can be successful if they simply apply themselves and get a few lucky breaks. We live with false images of success dancing in our heads. We fantasize in order to relieve the humility and boredom of our creaturely existence.

When Christians feel the pressure of humble circumstances, their advisers and leaders often foster, rather than correct, their visions of success. Relief from feelings of self-depreciation is sought by moving with the prevailing winds of popular advice. Christians are counseled to become more attractive, successful, self-assertive and intimate. They are encouraged to dress better, diet more, vacation often and aim high.

Far from catering to the presumption that success is the Christian's inalienable right, James counsels perseverance in our humble circumstances. His advice runs against the grain of popular Christianity. A Christian in humble circumstances ought to take "pride in his high position." Self-worth and self-confidence do not depend on our circumstances, but on our relationship to God. The sooner false visions of success are dispelled the better.

Cut-Flower Success

"Disappointment with God," Philip Yancey writes, "does not come only in dramatic circumstances. For me, it also edges unexpectedly into the mundaneness of everyday life. . . . Petty disappointments tend to accumulate over time, undermining my faith with a lava flow of doubt. I start to wonder whether God cares about everyday details—about me."[1]

In an effort to stem the "lava flow of doubt," James corrects three misconceptions about God and three false expectations about the Christian life. Emotions can erupt against God (1) when we nurture false expectations of what he has promised, (2) when we blame him for our own sinful desires, or (3) when we despise his good gifts through ingratitude.

First, James addresses our strong tendency to equate human success with God's success. The gospel of health and wealth has sanctified this misconception and created the illusion of a "sugar-daddy" God. Ask whatever you want and you will receive, regardless of whether your desires conform to God's will. James sees this for what it is: denying the reality of humble circumstances and the necessity of persevering under trial. The Christians who received this letter were especially vulnerable to counterfeit excellence. References throughout the book of James show that he was writing during a period of economic and political instability (1:27; 2:5-7, 14-17; 5:1-7). The generous sharing of the early church described in Acts 2 had fallen out of style. Those with economic means must have grown reluctant to share. As Peter Davids observes, "Under financial pressure people tend to hold orthodox belief but also to grasp tightly to whatever money they have."[2] They may not have changed their statement of faith but they had altered their practice of "body life." Scarcity had triggered self-interest.

In a few short days, the beautiful cut flowers that adorn the casket in a funeral home wilt and are thrown away. Similarly, fortune and fame captivate the popular imagination, but quickly wither under the heat of real-life needs and struggles. Self-respect must be rooted in spiritual maturity and growth. To persevere in times of material need and economic insecurity, we must exchange envy for joy and an inferiority complex for confidence in God. James knows that we cannot face humble circumstances with pure joy if we are hooked on the world's value system. Therefore Christians who are materially poor need to measure their life and self-worth by what they have already received—the grace and mercy of Jesus Christ—and what they will receive—"the crown of life that God has promised to those who love him" (v. 12).

The rich, on the other hand, need to think of their low position. They must equate their wealth not with self-importance, but with the responsibility to meet the needs of others. They will profit from reflecting on and identifying with the sacrificial life of Christ.[3]

The world's value system can pay an athlete five million dollars a year to throw a football or an actor a million dollars to tape a thirty-second commercial. We all know that those who tap into the mass market strike gold, and this fact leads to wild discrepancies in rewarding people for their labor. But there are also great differences between professionals: many high-school teachers barely make twenty thousand dollars a year, while some university business professors clear ninety thousand. We could debate the law of supply and demand and the rewards for personal sacrifice, but our primary consideration is how the world's value system controls and manipulates self-esteem and self-worth in the body of Christ.

Compare the respect shown to a young executive in an ad agency with that shown to a nurse. The executive works long hours and under great pressure—all for the sake of a company that produces perfume. Ah, but the benefits: his salary can reach six figures. He drives a BMW equipped with car phone and vanity plates, lives in a luxury condo and has a posh health club membership. In January or February he appears in church sporting a tan fresh from a week in Florida. Once a year he flies to Aspen or Banff for a weekend of Alpine skiing. This executive's high salary and glitzy perks command respect from many people. He is even inclined to think more highly of himself and enjoy his success.

The nurse also works long hours, perhaps the 3-11 shift on a surgical floor five days a week and every other weekend. She faces constant pressure every night, as she bears responsibility for the very lives of patients who critically need medical attention. Physical and emotional stress, trauma and death are part of her daily routine. Yet she can only afford a modest apartment and struggles to make ends meet. Regardless of the human value of our vocation, we tend to measure its worth in dollars. We are socialized to buy into the symbols of status. As our spiritual director, James turns the world's value system upside down. He replaces the symbols of status with the crown of life.

The Evil Within

Second, James seeks to reverse the downward spiral of disappointment by confronting the evil within. The human capacity for self-deception is great. We can convince ourselves of almost anything if we are unwilling to face the truth about ourselves. We have a strong compulsion to reinforce our self-serving bias. With little provocation we can convince ourselves that God is actually setting us up for a fall. We become angry with our humble circumstances. God is to blame.

In subtle and not-so-subtle ways, some accuse God of being responsible for the temptations they encounter, as if it is God's fault that we live in a fallen and broken world. They carry on an inner monolog, rationalizing their actions by blaming God. If God didn't want them to do whatever is needed to get ahead in their career, he never would have given the job to them in the first place.

Some go so far as to blame God for their immoral actions. If God wanted them to remain sexually pure, they reason, he would not have given them such a strong sex drive. God never would have worked out such a good deal on a new home if he didn't want them to buy it. They act as if God is trying to frustrate them. "Why was I born with such a talented voice if I can't land a performing job?" If they are unsuccessful, it's God's fault. "Why is God blocking my acceptance into medical school?" The temptation is strong to grumble and complain like the Israelites did after their bondage in Egypt. Some even wonder if trusting God works at all. If it worked, wouldn't life go better than it does? Instead, they struggle with humble circumstances and evil desires. And they spiritualize the struggle by blaming God.

James warns that the downward spiral of disappointment and desire can land the unsuspecting believer in the graveyard of despair and death. There is a strong attraction to a lifestyle that is inconsistent with spiritual maturity. Where there ought to be a holy dissatisfaction with cut-flower success and evil enticements there is a compelling fascination. James puts us on alert. We need to guard against the easy deception of a self-serving ego and a pleasure-seeking will. Our disappointment with God is the product of our false expectations.

As a parent, I have a growing empathy for my heavenly Father. I realize that some of the things my children have said to me I have also said to God. For example, when my nine-year-old son misconstrues something I said I would do for him, he may say in wounded disbelief, "But you promised!" Or when I have asked my five-year-old daughter to clean up her room and she fails to do it, I have occasionally heard, "You didn't tell me!" And to the simple fatherly directive "It's bed time," I have heard all three of my children respond in unison, "That's not fair!"

But the fact is, I say the very same things to God. I want something so bad that I distort God's promises to fit my expectations. When my wish-dream doesn't materialize, I complain, "But you promised!" Or when my disobedience to the clearly communicated will of God becomes painfully apparent, I defensively try to excuse my actions by shifting blame: "You didn't tell me!" And there have been many times—too many to count—when I have overlooked, ignored, even despised God's good gifts and insisted on complaining in my heart to him, "That's not fair!"

We are primarily interested in our success; God is interested in our spiritual maturity. We want special attention; God wants to give us spiritual direction. We feel humiliated by our humble circumstances; God sees the blessing of perseverance. We want to take whatever we can get; God wants us to receive "the crown of life." We want to turn our lives into a parade of self-achievement and self-expression; God wants to give us wisdom.

Good Gifts

Finally, our spiritual director understands the value of God's parenting and the process of true maturity. James refuses to sell out to worldly values, cheap desires and bogus perspectives. He is aware of the downward spiral of disappointment and seeks to reverse the momentum. Therefore he challenges us to face our trials joyfully and confidently for the sake of a deepening relationship with God. He insists that we persevere in our humble circumstances, remain aware of our "high position" in Christ and resist temptation honestly, without self-incriminating charges against God.

James touches on a lot of negative issues, but from a positive perspective. His opening counsel, "Consider it pure joy, my brothers, whenever you face trials of many kinds," moves to the beautiful and powerful affirmation that "every good and perfect gift is from above" (v. 17). The prayer for wisdom (v. 5) is a reminder that "all prayer, pursued far enough, becomes praise."[4] We are deceived if we think the Christian life is all trial and testing. God's great goodness is woven into the texture of daily life. Humankind, made in the image of God, pulsates with the joy of friends and family. Creation is brimming with God's good and perfect gifts. Yes, there are shadows of doubt and dark clouds of pain and suffering, but the sunshine of God's blessing does break through. Light will not be denied. Darkness comes to an end. James reminds us that God "chose to give us birth through the word of truth, that we might be a kind of firstfruits of all he created." In Christ we are born into a new world of truth and life. The world as God meant it to be is being restored and we are the "firstfruits" of that restoration. Instead of bemoaning our many trials and our humble circumstances, we who are born anew through the Word of Truth can take hold of incomparable goodness and inextinguishable joy. God's good and perfect gifts overcome the evil trials and temptations.

*He chose to give us birth through the word of truth,
that we might be a kind of firstfruits of all he created.*

*My dear brothers, take note of this: Everyone should be
quick to listen, slow to speak and slow to become angry, for man's anger does not bring about the righteous
life that God desires. Therefore, get rid of all moral
filth and the evil that is so prevalent and humbly accept the word planted in you, which can save you.*

*Do not merely listen to the word, and so deceive
yourselves. Do what it says. Anyone who listens to the
word but does not do what it says is like a man who
looks at his face in a mirror and, after looking at
himself, goes away and immediately forgets what he
looks like. But the man who looks intently into the
perfect law that gives freedom, and continues to do
this, not forgetting what he has heard, but doing it—he
will be blessed in what he does.*

*If anyone considers himself religious and yet does not
keep a tight rein on his tongue, he deceives himself and
his religion is worthless. Religion that God our Father
accepts as pure and faultless is this: to look after
orphans and widows in their distress and to keep
oneself from being polluted by the world.*

JAMES 1:18-27

5
FROM
PERFORMANCE
TO
WORSHIP

THERE is a "back-to-the-basics" quality about James's spiritual direction. We don't need new insights as much as we need a fresh reminder of basic truth. Under the pressure of daily life, with our ingrained habits and personality weaknesses, the vital concerns and important priorities are lost. Authentic Christian faith, slowly built up by the disciplines of grace—worship, prayer, service and witness—quickly turns to religious flab when faith and practice are no longer seriously held together.

Casual Christianity turns religion into an excuse for self-expression, good intentions and free-wheeling opinions. James warns his dear friends that the end product of careless anger, spectator spirituality and a loose tongue is counterfeit Christianity. The very things we are inclined to overlook, James attacks head on. We have grown so accustomed to self-righteous anger, do-nothing piety and back-biting gossip that we hardly notice the problem. We have lived with these ordinary sinful habits for so long. But our spiritual director puts down the things we put up with.

We find these problems too difficult to get a handle on. Adultery "automatically" calls for church discipline, but when a member erupts in a rage over the selection of a hymn, he or she is ignored. Swearing in most Christian circles calls for censure, but saying one thing and doing another is commonly accepted. Drunkenness brings immediate repercussions, but manipulative church politics is accepted as a fact of life. Old evil habits die hard. They are stubbornly resistant to sanctifying grace. But that does not excuse their practice, much less encourage their replacement with positive habits. It takes a prophet-pastor to forcefully remind us of how we are meant to be.

The Sacrifice of Fools

Christians can easily forget who they really are and deceive themselves. Lying can take many forms. There are bold-faced lies and there are finely crafted false impressions. We can withhold just enough truth to mislead, or slant the truth in order to deceive. We are commanded not to lie—not to our children, not to our colleagues, not to our spouse, not even to strangers and enemies. Why then do we lie to ourselves?

"Self-deception is a fine art," Lewis Smedes writes. "It is a balancing trick in which we hover between knowing and refusing to know. In one corner of our mind we know something is true; in another we deny it. . . . We see it for just an instant, long enough to feel its threat, and we close it off. We 'know,' but we refuse to know."[1] "Ignoring isn't the same as ignorance," Margaret Atwood has written, "you have to work at it."[2]

Three times James admonishes believers to stop hovering between knowing and refusing to know:

Don't be deceived, my dear brothers. Every good and perfect gift is from above. . . .

*Do not merely listen to the word, and so deceive yourselves. Do what
it says. . . .*

*If anyone considers himself religious and yet does not keep a tight rein
on his tongue, he deceives himself and his religion is worthless.*

The root cause of this self-deception stems from knowing the truth but
refusing to live by it. We know about God's good gifts and his revealed
word in theory. The truth sounds good in a sermon and looks right
in print. But practically speaking, we pursue self-interests, do our own
thing, and say whatever we think whether it is true and edifying or not.

We instinctively turn away from what we find ugly in ourselves. We
are like the man in Jesus' parable who spotted a speck of dust in the
other man's eye but was blind to the beam in his own eye. We find
it terribly difficult to come to terms with our own racial prejudice and
critical spirit. Among our Christian friends we adhere to an unwritten
rule: "If you don't find anything wrong with me, I won't find anything
wrong with you." We sing about how "Amazing Grace" has "saved a
wretch like me," but just let anyone suggest we've done something
wrong, and we'll hold a grudge against them for months.

When Ginny and I lived in a one-bedroom apartment in Toronto,
we had a problem with cockroaches. Late at night I would go into the
kitchen, flip on the light and see these creatures scurry across the floor
or counter. A light sleeper by nature, I developed a nocturnal habit of
hunting down cockroaches at 3 A.M. and killing as many as I could.
After some weeks, I realized that this was an odd activity for a graduate
student to be doing in the middle of the night. And Ginny didn't
particularly enjoy waking up each night to my banging around in the
kitchen. So I decided I had played around long enough. It was time to
get serious about my problem and find out where all these cockroaches
were coming from.

What I discovered amazed me. I had never noticed a small opening
between the top of the kitchen cupboard and the ceiling, only twelve
inches from eye level. In that crack were literally hundreds of
cockroaches, nesting right above our food! My nightly antics were

nothing more than playing with the problem. We had to clean everything out of the kitchen and call in an exterminator. When I am tempted to deal lightly with my sin, I remember how I deceived myself into thinking that knocking off a few cockroaches a night would solve the problem. Sometimes we only play at eradicating sin. We know it's there and we stomp on it occasionally, but we don't deal with its source.

Deception paves the way for disobedience. By willfully ignoring the truth, sinful habits such as anger and apathy go unchallenged. It takes real effort to separate what God has united. Faith and practice belong together, but many have managed to hold to one and despise the other. Great effort is now expended to make the application of God's truth inscrutable. Obedience falls victim to a thousand distractions and qualifications. Christianity becomes hypocritical, a religious abstraction. It may still consist of services, programs and committee work, but it is worthless.

Hypocrisy is difficult only in the sense that we must actively ignore the obvious application of truth. We subject God's truth on marriage, money, meaning and missions, to name just a few, to the court of public opinion, pious pretense and personal preference. Ignoring is hard work. It takes clever Scripture twisting, undisciplined zeal and shallow thinking to separate religion from obedience. But in the end disobedience is hardly any work at all. It flows naturally from deception. Having done the work of ignoring, we easily fall into hypocrisy. But hypocrisy is also a great affliction, a tiresome ordeal. It is a burden borne by those who want enough Christianity to make themselves feel good, but not enough to change their lives. But the Christian life cannot mature under the pretense of religious performance.

Offering a message very similar to James, the writer of Ecclesiastes warned: "Guard your steps when you go to the house of God. Go near to listen rather than to offer the sacrifice of fools, who do not know that they do wrong" (5:1). Many people mistake religious experience and church involvement for the Christian life. They become addicted to their own enthusiasm for the superficial and cling to empty sentiment. They plan a church wedding but do not prepare for Christian marriage. They mouth the words of hymns but sing without heartfelt praise. They wax eloquent about vision and outreach. They are filled with dreams of success. They assume that the entrepreneurial spirit of the marketplace works well in evangelism. They set numerical goals, plot evangelistic strategies, attend marriage seminars, raise building funds and offer the sacrifice of fools.

"Do not be quick with your mouth, do not be hasty in your heart to utter anything before God. God is in heaven and you are on earth, so let your words be few. As a dream comes when there are many cares, so the speech of a fool when there are many words" (Eccl 5:2-3).

God does not suffer fools. We may deceive ourselves, but we cannot deceive him. We need less hype and more holiness. And most of all, we need less self-assertion and more humility.

Humble Acceptance
The best protection against deception is the Word of God. Each time James warns against deception, he commends the word of truth and freedom. The secret to life is found not in making a life for ourselves, but in receiving the truth and wisdom offered by God. The temptation to live in the past, with its sinful cravings, evil lusts and egotistical boasts still dogs believers even though they have been born into a new realm. Those who have experienced new birth must learn how to live all over again or choose to remain in perpetual infancy.

The analogy of the new birth is a telling one. None of us had a say in our natural birth. We did not choose to be born nor lobby our parents for a place on the family roster. Even though we didn't cast a vote, we were not the products of fate or chance. Decisions were made, independent of us, that brought us into existence. Like it or not, we are the product of those decisions. We began this life of decision-making and individuality rather passively. Since our lives have been and continue to be subject to the decisions of others, we should pause and reflect on the language James uses to describe this second birth:

"He chose to give us birth through the word of truth, that we might be a kind of firstfruits of all he created" (1:18).

The power of choice, as far as James is concerned, lies with God. He chose to give us birth. We are on the receiving end of God's grace and mercy. This does not deny the equally important truth of our responsibility toward God nor our decision for God, but it places the human will squarely in the context of God's grace. We have begun a new life, shaped and nurtured by the word of truth. We need to receive rather than achieve.

Ginny and I have three children—two adopted and the third unexpected. Each one a special surprise and a great delight! Not only did our children have no say in who would be their parents, but we felt we had little say in becoming parents. We *wanted* to be parents and we expressed that desire in the adoption agency interviews with social workers, but the real decision belonged to God. Whether we had children was God's choice, not ours. We could not become parents on our own; we could only receive God's sovereign care. This picture also illustrates my new birth in Christ. God's choice is the ultimate reason for my decision for Christ.

When I first held Jeremy, I couldn't get over the helplessness, the utter dependence, of a newborn infant. He was almost too fragile to hold, a priceless bundle of life that in almost no time (if you don't count sleepless nights) grew into a stocky, unbreakable sixth-grader. Children grow stronger physically, but they remain pretty vulnerable emotionally and relationally. For years they are dependent spiritually. They require daily nurture and consistent discipline. Anyone can give them food and shelter, but it takes a special care-giver to cultivate truth and plant the seeds of justice and mercy. I don't want to simply expose them to truth or indoctrinate them in truth, I want them to grow up in the truth. I want the roots of truth to sink deep down into their character.

The language of birth emphasizes how radical this new life in Christ was meant to be, and how much we need to receive in order to live it. We don't move from infancy to adulthood overnight. Wisdom and maturity are cultivated over time and through much perseverance, prayer and testing. To be born again through the word of truth is to submit our wills to the parenting of our heavenly Father. We undergo, by choice, a reeducation in a Christian world-and-life view. We allow our lifestyles to be reshaped and our friendship lines to be redrawn. Old patterns of work and leisure change, permitting life to be renewed and restored in the direction God intended.

Quick to Listen, Slow to Speak
Humble acceptance of the implanted Word of God requires willed passivity. The noise and confusion of the rat race must be intentionally put aside. The ordinary sin of perpetual motion will not flee without our disciplined determination. The packed appointment schedule becomes proof of self-importance in a society that prides itself on being busy. The car phone is a status symbol; the crowded office, reassuring. By being "in demand" and "staying in touch," we feel wanted and needed, like Linus with his security blanket. We have equated busyness with importance for so long that we have forgotten how to contemplate truth and meditate on the Word of God. Unless we are on the run, we feel disabled.

It is almost comical—if it weren't so sad—to watch some people come to church. The worship service might as well be a sporting event. The call to worship and opening hymn are treated like the opening preliminaries of a basketball game before the buzzer. They are so accustomed to running around, arriving late, leaving early that they have no patience for quiet preparation. They make up an audience of busy people, who need music and sermons especially designed to distract them from their preoccupations. In the absence of self-discipline and personal devotion, worship is something done for people and to people. The extent of people's willed commitment to worship amounts to showing up fifteen minutes late, rushing to a seat and studying the bulletin.

The ability to listen is in short supply wherever distractions abound. Yet many of these distractions result from superfluous activities that can be easily cut out and electronic devices that can be simply turned off. A little self-discipline would go a long way in giving the spiritual disciplines a chance to grow. Turning the television off and slowing down the pace of life are practical remedies. They offer a simple solution for creating more space and time for truly hearing the Word of God. And compared to the distractions which concern James, they are easy to control and correct.

Anger

There is nothing quite like anger to absorb our attention and distract us from the implanted Word. When anger rushes in, "listening flies out," according to Alec Moyter.[3] Virtually any pastor can identify someone in the congregation on Sunday morning who is sitting in the pew fuming about something. The prophet Jeremiah was warned not to let the faces of the people discourage him. Their anger not only prevented them from hearing the Word of God, but threatened to intimidate the prophet. Anger erects an impenetrable wall, and even well-delivered truth ricochets off.

Why did James find it necessary in his spiritual direction to highlight this emotional distraction? Is he preparing some of the believers for the strong words to follow? Possibly. His concern is to encourage a thoughtful hearing of God's Word. He is not interested in a knee-jerk, emotional reaction. The purpose of good preaching and teaching is not to make people angry, but to help "bring about the righteous life that God desires" (Jas 1:20). Anger, "impregnated with sin—self importance, self-assertion, intolerance, and stubbornness" destroys both communication and contemplation.[4] If either the communicator or the hearer is filled with anger, there is little chance that the Word of God will come through faithfully.

Anger betrays a stubborn spirit, intent on having its own way. Unchecked, it grows into intractable rigidity and slow-burning bitterness. Festering anger spreads to others, inflicting on their souls the dreadful inability to hear and respond to the Word of God. While on the surface the issue may seem harmless—a passing remark, a hymn selection, a cold sanctuary—the underlying causes of anger may be deeply rooted grief, despair and selfishness.

Several years ago I was leading a song of praise in a midweek prayer meeting. We were singing Sydney Carter's "Lord of the Dance" to an old Shaker tune. As we came to the end of the song, we were startled by one of our deacons, who had slammed his songbook to the floor. His face red with rage and his eyes flashing, he literally yelled that we had no business singing a song about dancing. He then proceeded to condemn the song and us for singing it. I looked around and saw that everyone's face was red, not from anger but from embarrassment. I forget now what I said, but I didn't argue with him. I just wanted to move from his outburst to our usual meditation on a Psalm.

Several days later when I went to his home, I learned an important lesson about anger. He greeted me at the door and invited me into the living room. We sat down in silence. He placed both hands on the armrest of his chair, as if he were about to take off, and looked out into space. Then he took a deep breath, looked straight at me and said, "I suppose I should tell you about myself. I have to take early retirement because I can't handle the high-school kids any more. The parents are complaining, and the principal wants me out. I have enough sick-leave to carry me to retirement."

Obviously, the pressure he was under had brought him close to the breaking point. His anger over the song was touched off by far greater concerns troubling his life. For months he had been in emotional pain. We never did refer to the song or his outburst. We prayed together. I tried to comfort him. That afternoon I learned that often the issue that triggers an angry outburst has little to do with the real issues robbing us of peace.

It is easy for us to allow our anger and frustration to get in the way of hearing the Word of God. In so doing we cut ourselves off from the source of wisdom we need. Self-righteous pet peeves can get in the way of open, prayerful reflection on the Word of God. What James intended to be helpful instruction may be misconstrued as an insult. If we are not careful, we can become like the older son in the parable of the prodigal son. He was unable to appreciate his father's love and enter into the joy of his brother's return. His narrow-minded, dutiful religion replaced the open-minded maturity of the perfect law of liberty. I have acted like the disgruntled older brother many times. My self-justifying, self-serving work ethic has crowded out my appreciation for God's ongoing work of grace in the lives of people I would prefer to give up on. No wonder I find it difficult to hear what my heavenly Father is saying.

The Perfect Law
Humbly accepting the implanted Word means more than merely listening to the Word. There is little to be gained by religiously overhearing the Bible the way people listen to music in a department store. What passes for the voice of God in many churches may be little more than religious jargon and pious atmospherics. After years of repetitious sermons and perfunctory Bible readings, some people have become immune to the life-shaping power of God's Word. The Word is never allowed to penetrate a religious veneer.

One friend of mine spent twenty years listening to sermons and attending Sunday school classes before he began taking the Bible seriously. He admits now that the Bible had virtually no impact on his business career. It was a book of idealistic platitudes and pious sayings. He politely respected its aura of sacred importance, but found it hopelessly impractical for succeeding in the work-place. Only after a serious car accident and some deep soul-searching did he wake up to the practical significance of the Bible for daily living. Slowly he began to internalize the Word of God.

In obedience to the Word, he began changing the way he did

business. His priorities and values were transformed. His family became more important to him than his career. He altered his old habit of slanting the truth to make himself and his department look better. For years he had been able to sell customers more technology than they needed, thinking that if they were foolish enough to fall for his sales pitch, too bad for them. Now he could no longer do that. He found himself persuading customers to buy less rather than more, depending on their need. The symbols of status became less important. He tried to befriend people in the company whom he had previously disliked. He sought to rectify injustices which in the past he would have ignored or condoned. In short, he began living for the kingdom of God instead of the corporation. The mix of secular values and religious piety which had existed for so many years was no longer possible.

My friend's past was like that of the person described by James who, after looking at himself in the mirror, immediately forgot what he looked like. His understanding of the Bible never penetrated his self-absorbed little world of dreams and strategies. Biblical truth went in one ear and out the other, like computer data lost because he never punched the "save" key. He deceived himself into thinking that he was a fine upstanding Christian, when in fact he suffered a terrible case of spiritual amnesia when he left church.

There is no substitute for personal application of the Word of God. The language employed by James emphasizes the organic nature of true spiritual growth. We are born again through the word of truth. The implanted Word takes root. God's Word becomes a part of us—giving life, saving from death, offering freedom. We are like the prophet Ezekiel, who was enjoined to eat the scroll and fill his stomach with the Word of God (Ezek 3:1-3). The covenant promise to Jeremiah is fulfilled: "I will put my law in their minds and write it on their hearts. I will be their God, and they will be my people" (Jer 31:33).

True Religion
Controlling your tongue, looking after orphans and widows, and

keeping your body sexually pure is hardly the world's idea of freedom. It is not what most Christians think of when they think of freedom. To most people, achieving freedom and learning service belong on two different agendas. Freedom means freedom to do what I want to do whenever I want to do it. Service means serving the real needs of others. Freedom means having no burdens and responsibilities. Serving means owning those burdens and responsibilities.

In the popular imagination, freedom and service are achieved differently. Their paths seldom cross. They are two goals at opposite ends of the field. But in true spiritual direction, freedom and service are achieved together. In their true form they simply cannot be pulled apart since they are bonded together by the grace of God. The ancient equation still stands: "Whoever wants to save his life will lose it, but whoever loses his life for me will find it" (Mt 16:25). We have to give ourselves away to gain freedom, and we have to serve others to know liberty. God's law and human liberty belong together. Costly service and true freedom are united.

True religion may sound more like a burden than the blessing James promises (1:25). It is indeed burdensome if we are unwilling to receive what "the Father of heavenly lights" desires to give. Wisdom, peace and freedom, three blessings of the Christian life, will remain elusive ideals for anyone who refuses to humbly receive and obey the word of truth. The Giver of "every good and perfect gift" calls us to give ourselves away to the orphan and widow. In doing so we understand the perfect law of liberty.

Eugene Peterson writes: "The great danger of Christian discipleship is that we should have two religions: a glorious biblical Sunday gospel . . . and an everyday religion that we make do with during the week."[5] Everyday religion, with its small cliques, personal preferences and petty grievances, crowds out true religion. And when this happens, the next generation grows up rejecting what it thinks is the Christian faith, but is in fact a worthless copy. For all practical purposes the children of a lost generation of religionists have never seen authentic Christianity at work. James, our prophet-pastor, wants to save us from the burden of spiritual presumption, self-deception and hypocrisy. Through the perfect law of liberty he leads us back to the often-neglected fundamentals of the faith, such as humbly receiving the implanted Word and serving orphans and widows.

My brothers, as believers in our glorious Lord Jesus Christ, don't show favoritism. Suppose a man comes into your meeting wearing a gold ring and fine clothes, and a poor man in shabby clothes also comes in. If you show special attention to the man wearing fine clothes and say, "Here's a good seat for you," but say to the poor man, "You stand there" or "Sit on the floor by my feet," have you not discriminated among yourselves and become judges with evil thoughts?

Listen, my dear brothers: Has not God chosen those who are poor in the eyes of the world to be rich in faith and to inherit the kingdom he promised those who love him? But you have insulted the poor. Is it not the rich who are exploiting you? Are they not the ones who are dragging you into court? . . .

If you really keep the royal law found in Scripture, "Love your neighbor as yourself," you are doing right. But if you show favoritism, you sin and are convicted by the law as lawbreakers. For whoever keeps the whole law and yet stumbles at just one point is guilty of breaking all of it. . . .

Speak and act as those who are going to be judged by the law that gives freedom, because judgment without mercy will be shown to anyone who has not been merciful. Mercy triumphs over judgment!
JAMES 2:1-13

6

FROM
FAVORITISM
TO
FRIENDSHIP

WHEN we enter the household of faith, we long to feel the joy expressed by the psalmist: "I rejoiced with those who said to me, 'Let us go to the house of the Lord' " (Ps 122:1). The joy of worship, nurtured in the shared experience of friendship, requires setting aside the relational strategies of preferential treatment and pragmatic self-interest. True friends need not compete with each other to gain the upper hand. The church should be a competition-free zone.

Spiritual direction seeks to release believers from the profit motive, the order of appearances and the politics of friendship. Sabbath worship is a welcome respite from the office pecking order, the flirting and flattery of the world's daily routine. In the household of faith, friendship begins with a call to worship the Lord God. Stroking egos gives way to praising God. Mercy overcomes manipulation. The Lord's Supper replaces the power lunch. Instead of courting one another's favor we rejoice in God's favor.

Sizing People Up

The problem is that the way we operate all week does not dust off easily on Sunday. Without spiritual direction and purposeful resistance, we fall back into the habits of human nature and custom. Christian service turns into customer service, and favoritism evaluates every relationship in terms of profit or loss. We size people up. We are as sharp as Sherlock Holmes in spotting the telltale signs of prominence, prestige, influence, control.

Ironically, we reject some of the very people who have the most to offer simply because they don't meet our standard of "cool." One Indiana University music student whom I have counseled claims to have nothing to live for but her violin playing. She feels painfully alone and empty. Her six to eight hours of daily practice in a small, soundproof cubicle compound her feelings of isolation. She tried several sexual relationships and the bar scene in a vain attempt to find friendship. But this brought no relief; it only heightened her anxiety. I suggested that there were some mature Christians in the music school who were striving to integrate their musicianship with their faith in Christ. She agreed, but then said they wouldn't really make good friends. "Why?" I asked.

"Because they're nerds," she replied. "They're just too good to be real; they're sort of odd. They aren't as competitive as I am. They're too nice. I'm a real music jock."

"But it doesn't sound fair to yourself or to them," I said, "to reject their friendship because they are good. I could understand it if you thought they were hypocrites. But it sounds like you are dismissing them because they are authentic."

She shrugged her shoulders. "I know, but that's just how I am." Having accepted the music school's unwritten code of prestige and ranking, she snubbed the very people who could truly befriend her. Christians were not cool enough to be seen with. She was embarrassed to be with them, even though they offered a way of living that she needed. The problem of sizing people up for personal advantage is old, but the practice is ever new. As discriminating consumers, we do in the church what the car dealer, real estate broker and retailer do in the marketplace. According to James, we judge one another with evil thoughts. We prostitute worship and friendship for the sake of making a favorable impression. James's spiritual direction is simple and emphatic: "Don't show favoritism!" At first glance, James's parable may appear irrelevant. The wealthy don't always dress up for church today; they may dress down. They would no sooner want to parade to the front of the sanctuary than be called on to take the offering. (Seats at the ball game may be another story.) The issue is not the dramatic entrance, but the powerful influence prominent people exert within the church. And this matter is quite relevant to our Christian maturity; it illustrates just how practical spiritual direction can be. When favoritism takes a front-row seat, friendship sits in the corner.

Emotional Blackmail

Why does the wealthy man in James's story receive special attention? There are several possible answers. Perhaps the one who led this prominent man to his seat of privilege was in the habit of catering to the wealthy every business day. He may have thought: Why should a worship service be any different from the workplace? What makes the house of God different from the office? Force of habit may provide sufficient reason for this customary deference. The rules of the game are played out seven days a week, making the Christian community a mere extension of the world. But habit alone is only part of it. There are other contributing factors.

Insecurity also plays a role. We are afraid of what powerful, prominent people will think of us and our church if they are not treated in a special way. We are susceptible to favoritism when we lack the confidence of Christian friendship. The man ushered to the best seat is not so much a brother in Christ as a man of means and influence. We are intimidated by his presence, afraid we might say or do the wrong thing. If we slip up, we may hear about it from him later. We have learned that it is important to stay on the good side of demanding personalities. Insecurity causes us to give in to their forceful, pretentious ways. Pressured by our feelings, we manage their egos according to their expectations.

Perhaps the "usher" in James's parable knew the wealthy man would have left in a huff if he had not received special attention. Favoritism is pragmatic. It works. People are stroked, egos are satisfied, and the building program is financed. Those receiving special treatment expect it, and those giving it feel obliged to do so. Favoritism is calculating, manipulative and burdensome.

A Friendly Church

Our spiritual director does not advise us to treat everyone like a VIP. The problem for James is not that the poor man is told to sit in the corner. That is wrong, of course, because it discriminates. But even if there were no poor man, it is still evil to slant one's criteria toward the prominent and influential. Many well-heeled churches have no poor to slight, but they fall into the trap of favoritism just the same. Friendship determined by favoritism distorts and displaces what ought to be important between friends. Virtues of honesty, patience, faithfulness and forgiveness are replaced by the attractions of the sinful nature. Favor belongs to those who are important to be seen with, whose lifestyle is enviable, whose connections are impressive. To win their favor concessions must be made. Sociability tends to become more important than spirituality. Being known as a "friendly, dynamic church" outpaces the importance of worship, and good PR ranks above a prophetic understanding of God's Word.

What people often mean when they speak of a friendly church is one that has finely tuned the art of favoritism. The visitor is treated like a customer who is shopping for a new church "home." A strategy is put in place so people feel welcome. Visitors are "handled" effectively and programs presented attractively. Friendliness is offered with an ulterior motive: to preserve the reputation of the church as warm and friendly and to make the newcomer a repeat customer.

We need an alternative to the burden of being a so-called friendly church. Managing the visitor's first impressions is not the same as offering true friendship. We may end up attracting people to ourselves, not Christ. When friendship is determined by favoritism, our "friends" end up becoming more trouble than they are worth. If we "handle" people like customers, is it their fault when they treat us like religious retailers? Favoritism distorts the meaning of friendship and service. The people we cater to end up exploiting us because we have fed their false expectations of how they should be served.

Christian Community

The good news is that spiritual direction offers an alternative. A growing Christian community can learn to demonstrate the difference between favoritism and friendship. Dietrich Bonhoeffer, a powerful twentieth-century spiritual director, has written: "The basis of all spiritual reality is the clear, manifest Word of God in Jesus Christ. The basis of all human reality is the dark, turbid urges and desires of the human mind. The basis of the community of the Spirit is truth; the basis of human community of spirit is desire." As long as human desire inspires and controls "fellowship," then true Christian community is in retreat. "Every human wish dream that is injected into the Christian community is a hindrance to genuine community and must be banished if genuine community is to survive." When Bonhoeffer speaks of human desire, he is referring not only to self-serving ulterior motives, but to any personal intention, no matter how "honest and earnest and sacrificial," that is imposed on the Christian community.[1] Self-promoted crusades, even for good causes, disrupt and weaken Christian community.

The problem of favoritism is broader than we might think. It applies not only to preferential treatment of people, but to preferential advocacy of personal desires. It extends from the special regard conferred on a wealthy person to the "good ideas" people persistently favor at the expense of Christian community. If I insist that worship services reflect my own musical tastes, or if I seek to control the church budget according to my own preferences, then I am showing favoritism.

In our family of five, everyone likes different foods. Our eleven-year-old loves pizza, while our five-year-old is content with a peanut-butter-and-jelly sandwich. Recently the family voted that we were having one of my favorite meals too often—baked chicken and mashed potatoes. I suppose I could argue that my preference is more nutritional than theirs, but it is obvious that everyone's reasonable tastes deserve consideration.

In our church, some would like to hear forty-five minutes of uninterrupted worship music on Sundays, and others would prefer nothing but an opening hymn and a message. Some insist upon alternative Christian schools, others push for home-schooling, while most favor sending their children to public schools. If we were merely a human community, we would probably organize ourselves around our special interests and fellowship only with those who agreed with us. But we are not a social club or special interest group; we are a Christian community centered in Christ.

"The more genuine and the deeper our community becomes," Bonhoeffer writes, "the more will everything else between us recede, the more clearly and purely will Jesus Christ and his work become the one and only thing that is vital between us."[2] This does not mean that as Christians grow in grace, they will all think alike and their differences will vanish. Instead of producing passivity or indifference, the Christian community forges a bond in Christ that allows for diversity without disunity.

God's Friends
True spiritual direction offers the constant reminder that genuine

friendship is centered in Christ. The old criteria of what makes a relationship profitable are gone. Favoritism has been canceled. As Paul said, "From now on we regard no one from a worldly point of view" (2 Cor 5:16). A truly friendly church does not court our favor by appealing to our special interests. It receives us in and through Jesus Christ. Anyone can take people and arrange them by their self-interests, but the church receives everyone and anyone, accepts their differences, their needs and their sins, and leads them to repentance, to worship, to Christ.

In the body of Christ programs don't pull people together the way the YMCA does on Saturday morning. Christ makes us his friends. "The New Testament language of friendship," Rodney Clapp writes, "is more that of abiding than of profiting. Its most likely metaphors for friendship are organic and agricultural rather than economic: the disciple does not 'invest' in friendship so much as he or she is 'grafted' onto the vine or participates in the body where friendship flourishes."[3]

Friendship is spontaneous, not mechanical. It cannot be manufactured; it must grow as we mature in worship, prayer and compassion. In the words of Jonathan to his friend David, "The Lord is witness between you and me, and between your descendants and my descendants forever" (1 Sam 20:42). At the heart of their friendship, Jonathan and David recognized the presence of God. The covenant-making God bore witness to their fidelity and brotherly love. The bond between them was stronger than family ties, royal rights and personal glory.

We are friends to one another because Christ chose us. He became our friend by laying down his life for us, and by revealing the will of his Father to us (Jn 15:9-17). Instead of living by favoritism's motto, "Love your neighbor for yourself," we obey the royal mandate for friendship, "Love your neighbor as yourself" (Jas 2:8). Instead of sizing up one another we sacrifice for one another. Instead of maneuvering for the best possible advantage, we give ourselves to one another for the sake of Christ.

James wants his readers to know that discrimination and preferential treatment violate the will of God as much as adultery and murder (2:8-11). God will hold us accountable, either for expecting or showing favoritism.

There is no freedom in favoritism, only the burden of hurt feelings, bruised egos and power tactics. Self-interest insists on imposing its own agenda on friendship, while the perfect law of freedom guides friendship in the disciplines of forgiveness, mercy and love. As a true spiritual director, James makes us aware of how acts of favoritism, no matter how small, betray our friendship with Christ and weaken Christian community.

Faith and Friendship
Favoritism in the church denies the mercy we have received in Christ. It is a form of faithlessness. Whenever practiced, it creates a tragic irony like that of the unmerciful servant in Jesus' parable, who pleaded with the king to cancel his huge debt, only to turn around and deny mercy to a fellow servant who owed him a tiny amount. God has no recourse but to show us the failure of our tactics and techniques. Where favoritism runs rampant, friendship centered in Christ cannot be experienced, let alone celebrated. From one little story in James's back-to-basics spiritual direction, we see many problems resulting from favoritism. Friendship defined by favoritism is not friendship at all, but a dreary relationship devoid of God's grace and mercy. James leads us to repent, not only for practicing preferential treatment in the church, but also for so easily assuming that we should operate by the world's strategies outside the church. In Christ the game of one-upmanship is over. Flattery, deception and emotional blackmail cease. We are released from the bondage of courting people's favor and inching our way up the corporate ladder by duplicity.

The perfect law of liberty sets us free to seek one another's forgiveness. Spiritual direction leads to confession. If I have told you in so many words or actions to sit in the corner, or if I have ignored your need and sent you away empty, I need to repent and ask your forgiveness. If I have courted your favor and shown you preferential treatment to get on your good side, I need to repent and ask for your forgiveness. I no longer want to encourage false and deceptive expectations and betray our friendship in Christ.

What good is it, my brothers, if a man claims to have faith but has no deeds? Can such faith save him? Suppose a brother or sister is without clothes and daily food. If one of you says to him, "Go, I wish you well; keep warm and well fed," but does nothing about his physical needs, what good is it? In the same way, faith by itself, if it is not accompanied by action, is dead.

But someone will say, "You have faith; I have deeds."

Show me your faith without deeds, and I will show you my faith by what I do. You believe that there is one God. Good! Even the demons believe that—and shudder.

You foolish man, do you want evidence that faith without deeds is useless? Was not our ancestor Abraham considered righteous for what he did when he offered his son Isaac on the altar? You see that his faith and his actions were working together, and his faith was made complete by what he did. And the scripture was fulfilled that says, "Abraham believed God, and it was credited to him as righteousness," and he was called God's friend. You see that a person is justified by what he does and not by faith alone.

In the same way, was not even Rahab the prostitute considered righteous for what she did when she gave lodging to the spies and sent them off in a different direction? As the body without the spirit is dead, so faith without deeds is dead.

JAMES 2:14-26

7

FROM
BAD
FAITH
TO
SAVING
FAITH

IT IS difficult to escape James's clear teaching on the subject of saving faith. Anyone who claims to be saved by faith needs to sit up and take notice of James's direct attack on "bad faith." His arguments quickly demolish easy believism and cheap grace. True spiritual direction insists that not just any faith will do.

Many Christians cling to a very limited understanding of evangelism. They stress the simple gospel message and little else: Jesus died for our sins and whoever accepts him as their personal Savior will have everlasting life. For them the gospel, the "evangel," consists almost exclusively of this simple salvation message directed to lost souls. They love to quote Paul's words, "I resolved to know nothing while I was with you except Jesus Christ and him crucified" (1 Cor 2:2).

Unfortunately, this narrow understanding of evangelism equates a shallow, bare-bones gospel message with evangelical faith. Evangelism is reduced to inviting people to church for a brief presentation of the gospel followed by an emotional appeal to make a decision.

This was not, however, the apostle Paul's evangelistic strategy. Instead, he spent years in difficult urban centers such as Corinth and Ephesus "arguing persuasively about the kingdom of God" (Acts 19:8).[1] Paul did not want masses of stillborn "converts." He wanted solid citizens of the kingdom who had made their decision to follow Jesus and to receive the fullness of his salvation—but only after understanding and owning what it meant to live under the lordship of Jesus Christ. When Paul declared "Jesus Christ and him crucified," he did not present an abbreviated gospel. He then went on to powerfully apply the cross of Christ to every dimension of the Christian's life in Corinth, from lawsuits to diet to sexual morality to worship.

James follows in Paul's rich apostolic tradition, refusing to separate solid evangelism from true spiritual direction. We have in James a mentor who guides us in the full meaning of saving faith.

Useless Faith

James puts the question to us as directly as possible: "What good is it to have faith without deeds?" He answers his own question three times, like a refrain: "Faith by itself, if it is not accompanied by action, is dead" (v. 17). "Faith without deeds is useless" (v. 20). "As the body without the spirit is dead, so faith without deeds is dead" (v. 26). Evidently, James believed that the Christians he was writing to were in danger of settling for bad faith.

Bad faith is the experience of betraying what we claim to live by. Within ourselves we know we are not what we ought to be, even though our verbal skills and performance rating may be outwardly impressive. Bad faith is a form of self-deception. It is evident whenever religious decorum takes precedence over a life-transforming faith.

The recipients of James's letter were substituting rhetoric for righteousness, convenience for unconditional faith, and pious conformity for Christlike subversion. When all was said and done, there was more said than done. The kingdom of God was all talk and no power. Salvation by faith must have been a favorite evangelistic theme in their church services and personal witnessing, but it had become a cliché, cited without comprehending its full meaning.

James is argumentative, almost combative, in objecting to this view. He writes with a passion. He is uncompromisingly tough on all forms of spiritual presumptuousness. He abandons popular appeal and refuses to play to the audience—though he does invent a debater to argue the other side of his indefensible position. But in no way is he rude or disrespectful. He is writing to brothers and sisters in Christ. Underlying his impassioned plea for genuine faith is a strong bond of kinship.

Useless faith is shown by polite well-wishers who cover up human need with nice words and good intentions. Like the prophet Amos, James despised the trappings of religion, complete with tax-deductible offerings, elaborate Christian education curricula and special concerts. No matter how much else was going on, if the needs of Christian brothers and sisters were going unmet, then the claim to saving faith was empty.

Useless faith is the faith of "orthodox" demons who believe everything there is to believe about God, but deny the faith. They shudder but do not repent. They live a lie rather than accept what they know to be true. Such is the faith of those who say, "Lord, Lord," but do not obey the will of Jesus' Father (Matt 7:21). They even drive out demons and perform miracles, but their faith is useless. Jesus' verdict remains: "Away from me, you evildoers!" (Matt 7:23). James stands in a long tradition when he denounces cheap grace and bad faith.

Cheap Grace

With these two illustrations—the brother in need and the demons who believe—James argues against easy believism and raises the issue of how faith and works are related. To realize that genuine salvation shows itself in costly service can be slow and difficult.

When I went away to college, my faith in Christ meant a great deal to me, but I knew little of the biblical meaning of justice. I had some sense of Jesus' kingdom ethic and his purposes for the household of faith. But then I read *The Cost of Discipleship* by Dietrich Bonhoeffer for a course in ethics. I was impressed with the radical nature of Christian commitment. To believe is to obey and to obey is to believe. There can be no separation between believing in Jesus and following Jesus. The path of obedience leads to the cross.

My understanding of evangelism began to change as Bonhoeffer showed me how many churches have distorted the great truth of justification by faith alone by turning it into a justification for cheap grace. Bonhoeffer wrote:

Cheap grace is the grace we bestow on ourselves. Cheap grace is the preaching of forgiveness without requiring repentance, baptism without church discipline, Communion without confession, absolution without personal confession. Cheap grace is grace without discipleship, grace without the cross, grace without Jesus Christ, living and incarnate.

Costly grace is the treasure hidden in the field; for the sake of it a man will gladly go and sell all that he has. It is the pearl of great price to buy [for] which the merchant will sell all his goods. It is the kingly rule of Christ, for whose sake a man will pluck out the eye which causes him to stumble, it is the call of Jesus Christ at which the disciple leaves his nets and follows him. . . . Such grace is costly because it calls us to follow, and it is grace because it calls us to follow Jesus Christ. It is costly because it costs a man his life, and it is grace because it gives a man the only true life. It is costly because it condemns sin, and grace because it justifies the sinner.[2]

Bonhoeffer and others opened my eyes and heart to what the Bible clearly taught about saving faith. God does not want a religious performance or a mere verbal assent to an idea. He wants a life commitment to "work out your salvation with fear and trembling" by the grace of the Lord Jesus Christ (Phil 2:12). Costly grace disrupts our comfort zones and lays before us a challenge we would never dream of accepting apart from the grace of Christ.

I saw something of the scope of this challenge by spending a summer in Colombia with the Wheaton College Student Missionary Project. What I had been exposed to in the classroom was reinforced by what was for me a dramatic cultural experience. There was nothing special about my job; I painted a home used by a missionary and accompanied him on evangelistic outreaches. But it was the first time I realized how holistic the gospel had to be in order to be faithful to Jesus Christ. We couldn't just pass out tracts to people in abject poverty. I felt the challenge of a global gospel and the crying need for biblical justice. The gospel needed to be presented as a way of life, not just a religious solution. Otherwise, apart from biblical communities practicing their faith in tangible, practical ways, the meaning of saving faith would be either misunderstood or ignored.

It was a new experience for me to walk down the street and hear "Yankee go home!" shouted at me. To my dismay, I stood out, by virtue of my appearance, as an "ugly American." This was a challenge to my cultural pride, a reminder that the only way out of such a negative image was through Christlike service. I didn't need to go so far from home to feel the burden of my cultural bias, but Colombia helped to break down my small-minded perspectives and cultural defenses. I became more Christian and less American.

During my time there I traveled with Bob Moyer, a missionary with South American Mission. He worked in the Sierra Nevada Mountains among the Kogi Indians. For me, Bob embodied the wisdom of James by caring for the Indians as he would a true friend. He ministered holistically—mind and body, soul and spirit. He enjoyed being with them. He worked at understanding their culture. He treated them for diseases and infections. He shared with them the saving gospel of Jesus Christ. Bob showed them his faith by his deeds and in the process offered me some unforgettable spiritual direction.

By God's grace I was beginning to better understand the grace of the Lord Jesus Christ and the relationship between faith and works. Faith in Christ is demonstrated through the works of faith. We are saved by faith alone, but saving faith is never alone. In the words of the Reformers, "Faith alone justifies, but not the faith that is alone." Works are meant to follow faith as sexual intimacy follows marriage, or as power flows from an energy source. "Men are not saved on account of any work of theirs," wrote Jonathan Edwards, "and yet they are not saved without works."

The apostle Paul affirmed the natural complement of faith and works when he wrote, "For it is by grace you have been saved, through faith—and this not from yourselves, it is the gift of God—not by works, so that no one can boast. For we are God's workmanship, created in Christ Jesus to do good works, which God prepared in advance for us to do" (Eph 2:8-10). Luther put it well: "True faith will no more fail to produce good works than the sun can cease to give light."[3]

Serving Faith

Faith without works is cheap grace. It is a useless, dead faith. Those who live by it are trusting in a religious illusion, a grace they bestow on themselves. To believers threatened by this delusion, James explained the true meaning of saving faith. He advocated three qualities of saving faith: service, sacrifice and subversion.

Serving faith accepts the personal responsibility to meet the needs of a brother or sister in Christ. Faith overcomes the inertia of indifference, the rationalizations, the unending calculations and the safe retreat into our own cocoon. Rhetoric without service destroys faith as quickly as any heretical idea ever could. Obviously James believed in the parable of the sheep and goats. The line Jesus drew between heaven and hell separated people by what they did or didn't do. Aiding "one of the least of these" was an act of faith.

Saving faith accepts the biblical definition of friendship: "This is how we know what love is: Jesus Christ laid down his life for us. And we ought to lay down our lives for our brothers." Faith gives birth to obedience. "If anyone has material possessions and sees his brother in need but has no pity on him, how can the love of God be in him?" Saving faith is responsive to the practical needs of others. "This then is how we know that we belong to the truth . . . " (1 Jn 3:16-17, 19).

Some Christians feel they have accomplished a great thing by simply identifying needs. Consciousness-raising becomes a substitute for personal involvement. Meeting people's needs gets bogged down by organizational bureaucracy, obscuring our true charge to act by faith. I have known churches that have painstakingly collected and dated canned food items for the needy, and then stored those cans for years without distribution. I have known church boards to invest thousands of dollars in stocks, and then appeal to the church for money to meet ministry needs. Spiritual direction exposes the duplicity of generating the appearance rather than the reality of service.

Serving faith makes our shared responsibility for one another a personal act of obedience. We do not wish to set up yet another committee that will demand more time and energy in looking at the need than in meeting it. We do not want to substitute good intentions for actions. Spiritual direction frees us up to deploy our resources in a more responsible and responsive way.

Sacrificial Faith

James illustrates the second quality of saving faith by appealing to the life of Abraham. From the humble brother in need to the father of biblical faith, James proves the significance of a working faith. Sacrificial faith, the kind exemplified in Abraham, accepts the responsibility to worship God unconditionally. The language of altar and offering employed by our spiritual director is significant. Abraham's worship took precedence over his feelings and expectations. The real world for Abraham was the world defined by the word and spirit of God. His life, with all of its hopes and dreams, bowed to the command of God, even when God asked him to do the unthinkable and sacrifice his son.

Abraham's act of sacrificial faith took place in private, observed only by God and Abraham's son, Isaac. At the heart of faith is the challenge to measure reality by the commands of God rather than the pleasures of the moment—or even by our deepest attachments.

Like the Reformers who recovered the doctrine of justification by faith, we need to recover the doctrine of worship by faith. The neglect of personal and corporate worship is a sign of cheap grace. If we are not careful, we could end up substituting the blessings of God for God himself. We pray for God's success at work. We ask him to bless our family. But then, work and family become more important to us than worship. Unlike Abraham, who was asked to give up his son—the very embodiment of the promise of God—we give up worship for trivial concerns such as television, sports and relaxation. We sacrifice the one thing that counts for many things that don't.

Sacrificial faith is unconditional faith. Nothing hinders the rhythm and pattern of life from centering on Jesus Christ. Not busy careers, hectic schedules, indifferent spouses, or the ebb and flow of feelings. The sacrifice is made on the altar of saving faith. By dying to self we live in the real world, the world of God's making and directing.

Subversive Faith

The third quality of faith identified by James is the subversive faith of Rahab. The brevity of her story and the obvious limitations of her theology did not dissuade either James or the author of Hebrews from stressing the importance of her faith. By placing Abraham and Rahab back to back, James is stressing that saving faith is no respecter of persons. There is no favoritism with God. Abraham, the father of Israel, and Rahab, a foreigner, came to God the same way. Abraham was commanded by God to sacrifice his son. Rahab was called upon to sacrifice her way of life.

Faith for Rahab meant betraying her world. It meant aiding the enemy and concealing the truth for the sake of the truth. It meant subverting her known world for an unknown world. She trusted in "the quiet power and creative influence of God's sovereignty"[4] and deceived the king of Jericho. Her situation did not afford her the luxury of indifference. She had to make up her mind to place her life in God's hands. Fear does not explain her motivation; faith does.

Subversive faith accepts the responsibility to be strong and courageous in a dying culture. Rahab's faith was the first example of daring faith the Israelites witnessed when they entered the promised land. This disreputable foreigner believed in the power of God. She knew that her life and culture were beyond repair. She needed deliverance. A new world was coming into being for Rahab, one that was truly livable. The scarlet cord was a symbol to God's people that the powers resisting God's work had already been subverted. Subversive faith means that the last will become first, and that the Jerichos of the world will be flattened.

The Faith of Jesus

As our spiritual director, James attacks the presumptuous reliance upon useless faith. It is faith in name only, devoid of righteous action and the power of the Spirit of God. Bad faith claims to accept Jesus, but refuses to follow Jesus. For James, salvation is by faith in the Lord Jesus Christ. But true faith in Jesus calls for the faith of Jesus. The two cannot be separated. The One who saves by faith alone shows all who are saved how to serve, sacrifice and subvert by faith for the glory of God. Through the life and ministry of Jesus, we see how salvation is worked out. We are not only saved from our sins, but we are "created in Christ Jesus to do good works, which God prepared in advance for us to do" (Eph 2:10). Christ alone can save us and propel us forward in a life of good faith. Saving faith is a serving, sacrificing, subverting faith. Only this faith will do.

Not many of you should presume to be teachers, my brothers, because you know that we who teach will be judged more strictly. We all stumble in many ways. If anyone is never at fault in what he says, he is a perfect man, able to keep his whole body in check.

When we put bits into the mouths of horses to make them obey us, we can turn the whole animal. Or take ships as an example. Although they are so large and are driven by strong winds, they are steered by a very small rudder wherever the pilot wants to go. Likewise the tongue is a small part of the body, but it makes great boasts. Consider what a great forest is set on fire by a small spark. The tongue also is a fire, a world of evil among the parts of the body. It corrupts the whole person, sets the whole course of his life on fire, and is itself set on fire by hell.

All kinds of animals, birds, reptiles and creatures of the sea are being tamed and have been tamed by man, but no man can tame the tongue. It is a restless evil, full of deadly poison.

With the tongue we praise our Lord and Father, and with it we curse men, who have been made in God's likeness. Out of the same mouth come praise and cursing. My brothers, this should not be. Can both fresh water and salt water flow from the same spring? My brothers, can a fig tree bear olives, or a grapevine bear figs? Neither can a salt spring produce fresh water.

JAMES 3:1-12

8
FROM
OPINION
TO
TRUTH

I F WE tend to think that sharing our opinions is a harmless exercise in self-expression, James has some thought-provoking, speech-arresting insights for us: Although faith without actions is dead, it may still be verbal. Lack of experience in faithful obedience does not seem to hinder people from leading Bible studies, setting church policies and expressing their opinion. But it should. In the mind of our spiritual director, there is a direct correlation between practice and discernment. If we don't use it, we lose it. Insight follows obedience. The kingdom of God consists not of talk but of truth.

Practical Heresies
James was especially concerned about how Christians were influencing

one another with their words. Instead of offering spiritual direction, they were promoting spiritual distortion. The truth about suffering, temptation, favoritism and obedience was becoming garbled by opinionated Christians. The weapon of influence identified by James was none other than the tongue. The power of words was undermining the truth and reinforcing popular misconceptions about the Christian life.

James combats many heresies, but not heresies of doctrine as much as heresies of practice. Most likely the churches' formal teaching was reasonably orthodox, but their practical teaching was heretical. Apparently people were influencing one another to reshape Christianity in their own image.

If anything, I feel we have made James's spiritual direction about taming the tongue too tame. We have missed the force of his teaching. We have domesticated his powerful words by concluding that we shouldn't be quite so outspoken. But James is not talking about being nice. He is not especially concerned about swearing or flattery or sarcasm. His concern lies with exposing false teaching and the popular misconceptions that destroy the integrity of the Christian life. People are presuming to speak for God when they have no business doing so. They are sharing their opinions rather than submitting to the Word of God. And the result is heresy—the heresy of neglecting the poor, playing favorites, blaming God for problems, spiritual apathy and ethical complacency. All of these, James argues, are being reinforced by the tongue.

The Temptation to Teach

As far as James is concerned, teaching has little to do with our popular notion of teaching. He is not envisioning formal, public speaking, the kind that goes on in a classroom or in a church on Sunday morning. His concern is more practical and comprehensive. He is troubled over what Christians teach one another through their offhanded comments, self-styled speculations and well-thought-out excuses. The desire to preach on Sunday morning may never have appealed to many who presume to be teachers, but the desire to influence others is nearly universal. We happily leave the preaching to the pastor, but we still want to have our say.

James is concerned about the opinionated teaching that goes on in a Bible study, around the dinner table or in a Sunday-school class. He puts a finger on our propensity to subject the truth of God's Word to our preconceived comfort zones. For James the question is whether our tongue serves the truth or serves our biases. Since the main thrust of James's direction here relates to how we influence one another, I feel that his opening warning against presumptuous, misguided teaching should be directly connected to his practical discussion of taming the tongue.

Personal Opinion

James's admonition touches upon the attitude we often bring to Bible study groups. It encompasses both how we offer and how we receive spiritual direction. In our eagerness to promote small groups, we may have unwittingly neglected our respect for the integrity of God's Word. "Getting into the Word" may be a euphemism for sharing our personal feelings. Instead of pursuing the discipline of centering our lives on Christ, through his Word, we may have preferred to dwell on our own needs and problems. If James were to sit in on our Bible study groups, how would he evaluate them? Better yet, how would it feel to belong to a Bible study led by James? Chances are we might do less talking and more listening.

Christians need a context for nurturing friendships and building relationships—a place to share needs, pray for one another and hold each other accountable. A small group Bible study is great for this, as long as the relational benefits are the fruit of serious reflection on the Word of God. I do not mean that Bible studies should be dry and boring, full of technical word studies, exegetical minutiae or esoteric philosophical analysis. Rather, I am advocating the kind of Bible study

James would approve of, where there is a shared attentiveness to the Word, leadership by gifted spiritual guides, relevant discussion and practical application. The focus of such a study is growing in Christ, not airing someone's personal agenda.

Personal opinion can easily dominate Bible studies of all kinds and all age groups. Older men may have met for years to rehash doctrinal issues such as predestination and free will; young mothers may share about their children and husbands; corporate types may discuss how Christ is good for business; university professors may dabble in controversial issues; college students may get together for an emotional lift; couples may want to talk about their marriages. The pressure is on to express yourself, give your opinion, share your feelings. But so often the immediacy of emotional relevance takes priority over the hard work of diligent study, reflection and listening.

How would we react if James were to write the same words to us that he wrote to those early Christians? We might say, "Who does James think he is to imply that his opinion is better than ours?" I am afraid that we would judge his criticism of our presumption as presumptuous. However, James felt no such qualms about stating his case boldly. He was convinced of his own teaching authority because it was rooted in God's Word and in God's call upon his life. According to James, presumption lies with those who assert their opinion over the revealed will of God, and then claim to speak for God.

The Power of Feedback

Electronic feedback in a sound system is something you want to eliminate. It is the annoying hiss or piercing squeal that hinders and competes with communication. Verbal feedback, on the other hand, tends to determine what is acceptable "truth" in most circles today. Instead of trying to eliminate personal opinion, we encourage it. When it agrees with our understanding, we accept it as truth, but when it differs, we dismiss it as mere opinion.

If Bible studies in the first century were turning into vehicles for self-expression, how much more in our own day, when public opinion holds so much clout, when popular "truth" follows trends rather than biblical precepts, and when the personal autonomy of the "me generation" sets the tone? "Ours is an age in which 'conclusions' are arrived at by distributing questionnaires to a cross-section of the population or by holding a microphone before the lips of casually selected passers-by in the street," writes Harry Blamires.[1]

Perhaps open-minded tolerance of everything and close-minded indifference to knowable, objective truth has influenced Christians far more than we realize. We have become so accustomed to looking upon convictions as personal possessions that we dismiss authoritative biblical preaching as the pastor's opinion. "In my opinion" is assumed, whether it is actually said or not. And "thus saith the Lord" is dropped. Faithful spiritual direction is easily dismissed when it does not coincide with personal tastes and preferences.

If truth can be distorted by popular opinion, then the forces that shape personal and public opinion have tremendous power over the truth. Marshall McLuhan's phrase "the medium is the message" means that how something is said is more important than what is said. In a culture that has grown up on publicity, advertising and entertainment, we tend to judge all communication according to our tastes. Style wins over substance.

We learn to dismiss much of what we hear through the media that we know is not true. But whether it is true matters less and less to us, because we are conditioning ourselves to receive messages simply as personal perspectives. All speakers speak for themselves, share their opinion, offer their own customized worldview. We consume communication as a product that only fills our time but not our minds. As we watch grossly overpaid personalities endorse products with words written by advertising copywriters, we come to suspect all forms of communication as biased and self-serving. We resolve to trust only our own opinion.

The opinionated person has difficulty humbly accepting the Word of God unless the feedback of personal preference and opinion can be turned off. Perhaps we could better understand what James meant if we changed his warning to read, "Not many of you should presume to be brain surgeons or airline pilots or computer programmers." Most disciplines require years of education and practical experience before someone can be said to be competent. Submitting to the knowledge of God requires a similar discipline and spiritual apprenticeship. There are no shortcuts to spiritual maturity. Careful interpretation and faithful practice result from discipline and the work of the Spirit of God. We are not competent to guide others in the Word of God until we have obediently submitted to the life-transforming power of God's Word.

Mouth Damage

The best way to shut off feedback is to control the tongue. For James this is no small issue; it is a major theme of his spiritual direction. The unleashed power of the tongue threatens the peace and joy of the household of faith. The battle of influence rages between the propaganda of self-appointed authorities and the truth of God's Word. James warns that the tongue is capable of a full range of evil, from boasting to blasphemy, from gossip to grumbling, from flattery to false witness. He calls the tongue "a world of evil" and "a restless evil, full of deadly poison." How we use our tongue reveals our character. It is an index of the heart. It mirrors our mentality and reveals our spirituality.

The tongue is used metaphorically, not only in what we say out loud, but also for what we say inside. The inner monologue of the soul shapes and reflects character. With our tongue we reinforce bitterness and arrogance. We not only disparage others, we despise ourselves. With silent words we deceive ourselves as well as others. Our tongue can function like the infamous Nazi propaganda chief Dr. Goebbels, brainwashing us of the truth. Even our unvoiced oaths against ourselves and others damage the soul.

In other words, the negative use of the tongue applies as well to the words we voice only to ourselves. These disparaging thoughts and damning words reinforce evil. They are self-destructive, wearing away at the soul and eroding our capacity for love and truth.

In the book of Proverbs the tongue and the heart are almost interchangeable metaphors for a person's character:

The tongue of the righteous is choice silver,
but the heart of the wicked is of little value. (10:20)
A man of perverse heart does not prosper;
he whose tongue is deceitful falls into trouble. (17:20)

The apostle Paul stressed the inseparable relationship of tongue and heart when he wrote, "For it is with your heart that you believe and are justified, and it is with your mouth that you confess and are saved" (Rom 10:10). Likewise Jesus stressed the connection between our words and our character: "The good man brings good things out of the good stored up in his heart, and the evil man brings evil things out of the evil stored up in his heart. For out of the overflow of his heart his mouth speaks" (Lk 6:45).

James knew that the tongue was a potent destructive force. He was not about to play down the catastrophic results of egotistical, opinionated teaching. He believed in the power of the tongue to corrupt the whole person and to set the whole course of life on fire.

To emphasize the uncontrollable nature of the tongue, James delivers a pile of graphic word-pictures: A simple bit controls the energy of a horse; a small rudder guides a ship with full sails; a small spark ignites a huge forest fire. Today we might add that a tiny computer microchip steers the space shuttle. Even though it's small, James declares, the toxic tongue is terribly difficult to control. It poisons the truth.

This Should Not Be!

By now James expects us to be convinced that the tongue is uncontrollable, totally corrupting and unpredictably perverse. Without a second thought Christians can say things that are completely out of character.

One minute they are praising "our Lord and Father," and the next they are cursing people "who have been made in God's likeness" (Jas 3:9). We are like the apostle Peter: one moment we confess, "You are the Christ, the Son of the living God," and the next moment we say, "Never, Lord!" (Mt 16:16, 22).

The more we are aware of the corrupting influence of the tongue, hopefully the more we will care about the integrity of God's Word. Silence does not cure the destructive power of the tongue. We are not told to hold our tongue, but to use our tongue wisely. James himself is a poor example of holding his tongue. One can hardly find a sharper, more confrontive tongue in the New Testament. The difference between the convicting tongue of James and the corrupting tongue of those who presume to teach and influence is that one speaks the Word of God and the other human opinion.

True spiritual direction cautions against a loose tongue and promotes personal humility and Christian charity. Our words need to be motivated and shaped by the word and spirit of Christ. We are often too hasty in drawing conclusions and claiming to know more than we do. It is difficult to admit we don't have all the answers.

As a seminary teacher, I occasionally met students who condemned any biblical interpretation that did not correspond to theirs. Coming from a narrow cultural background and a limited exposure to Christian thought, they wanted to argue and debate rather than to receive and listen. They presumed to teach their teachers. In their rush to take a position in every debate, they replaced a passion for Christ with polemics. Armed with opinions on everything from ethics to eschatology, they used their tongues as weapons to accuse and judge Christian brothers. Criticism can crowd out careful critical thought.

I have met a similar spiritual presumption in the church. Many well-intentioned Christians whose doctrines were formed at an impressionable time in their lives remain closed to any new insights from the Word. They sit in judgment on others by imposing their own standard of truth on the church. On Sunday morning, they make it their job to look for errors in the sermon. They seem more intent on hearing what's wrong with a message than hearing the Word of God. Such people are often difficult to get along with. Their presumption becomes an obstacle for spiritual growth, not only for themselves, but for those they influence. Their system of thought tends to become a substitute for knowing Christ.

Role Models

I could compile countless case studies of churches torn apart by the corrupting influence of the tongue, but it is more important to consider the people in our lives who have exemplified the teachable spirit and gracious attitude commended by James. They reveal the beautiful balance of conviction and humility, control and passion that we expect in a mature Christian and need in a spiritual director.

For many years I had the privilege of working at Ontario Theological Seminary under the guidance of Canadian theologian and church historian Ian Rennie. He modeled for me a humble openness to the often unpredictable work of the Holy Spirit among Christians. He taught me to hesitate before being critical of others and to consider believers more from God's perspective than from my own limited experience. Sometimes Ian's magnanimous spirit silenced my small-mindedness. His exemplary combination of biblical integrity and Christian charity was easily observable on a daily basis. On occasion I have seen Ian, like James, issue a few well-chosen words to arrogant believers who have presumed to teach and lead beyond their understanding. When I think of what it means to have a "teachable spirit," I reflect on Ian's receptiveness to the insights of Christian students who were much less knowledgeable than himself. Without ever being designated as such, Ian Rennie continues to serve me as a faithful spiritual director. James, I believe, would have enjoyed Ian's company and commended his example.

*Who is wise and understanding among you? Let him
show it by his good life, by deeds done in the humility
that comes from wisdom. But if you harbor bitter envy
and selfish ambition in your hearts, do not boast about
it or deny the truth. Such "wisdom" does not come
down from heaven but is earthly, unspiritual, of the
devil. For where you have envy and selfish ambition,
there you find disorder and every evil practice.*

*But the wisdom that comes from heaven is first of all
pure; then peace-loving, considerate, submissive,
full of mercy and good fruit, impartial and sincere.
Peacemakers who sow in peace raise a
harvest of righteousness.*
JAMES 3:13-18

9

FROM
CONFUSION
TO
UNDERSTANDING

ONE fall Saturday morning I looked out the kitchen window at all the leaves in the back yard. "We have a problem," I said to my two sons.

They both looked at me as if to question my use of "we." "How should we tackle it?" I asked. Before they could say anything, I made a proposal. "I think in order for us to get a feel for the size of the problem, it would be good for you guys to count the leaves first."

"Dad!" Jeremy exclaimed, "Everything will be covered with snow by the time we finish counting all those leaves."

Some approaches to problems are pretty impractical, a waste of time—like counting leaves before you rake them up. We get so bogged down in analysis that we forget the real issue. It gets lost in a pile of extraneous detail. Truth is obscured by diversionary tactics and self-interests. We need a prophet-pastor like James to cut through the confusion and get to the real issue.

Who Is Wise?

Problem-solving is a major issue for Americans. Therapists, accountants, parents, managers, lawyers, negotiators, administrators and counselors see it as a major part of their job description. As our spiritual director, James is also concerned with problem-solving. His no-nonsense approach to the Christian life zeroes in on a number of perennial issues troubling the Christian community—neglect of the poor, self-deception, favoritism and the power of personal opinion. Ultimately James argues that the issue has to do with wisdom: worldly wisdom versus heavenly wisdom. At the root of community problems is the issue of character. These two paragraphs on wisdom lie between James's references to internal conflict within the church (3:9; 4:1). The source for these problems cannot be traced to difficult circumstances or doctrinal disputes, but to a fundamental conflict between foolishness and wisdom in the human heart.

James raises the fundamental question of spiritual direction: "Who is wise and understanding among you?" He is not asking us to judge others, but rather to conduct a personal inventory. Is there a self-evident, self-authenticating quality of goodness in our lives? Do we show by our humble actions that we have wisdom?

In understanding James's approach to problem-solving, we first need to figure out what he meant by "wisdom" and by the "good life." James uses so many words in these two paragraphs that could mean almost anything to today's media-conditioned observers. Take for instance the popular Bill Cosby TV show. In America's favorite morality play, the Huxtables are portrayed as an easygoing, fun-loving family. They are the epitome of American success and sensitivity, sophisticated urban professionals with just the right blend of style and substance. What family wouldn't like to be like the Huxtables—upper-middle-class affability and a roll-with-the-punches philosophy of life?

Viewers are left wondering where they can acquire such calm tolerance and secular sensitivity. Where is the source for their popular wisdom? Is it found in professional success and a sense of humor?

If we copy the Huxtable brand of wisdom, will we know how to solve our family problems? I am skeptical. Wisdom is not the sum of charm, cordiality, diplomacy and a winsome wit. Worldly wisdom, wisdom without God at the center, may appear attractive and appealing, but it is a poor substitute for the real thing. Thankfully, the Bill Cosby program does not showcase vulgarity, blatant immorality, violence and greed. But being nice, no matter how appealing, is not the same thing as being wise. The virtues espoused on the program are commendable, but the source of these virtues remains elusive.

In a world of sin and evil, how do we get to the source of true wisdom? How do we cultivate the virtues honored by Christian and non-Christian alike? The critical deficiency in the best of worldly wisdom is well expressed by C. S. Lewis:

Niceness—wholesome, integrated personality—is an excellent thing. We must try by every medical, educational, economic, and political means in our power to produce a world where as many people as possible grow up "nice"; just as we must try to produce a world where all have plenty to eat. But we must not suppose that even if we succeeded in making everyone nice we should have saved their souls. A world of nice people, content in their own niceness, looking no further, turned away from God, would be just as desperately in need of salvation as a miserable world—and might even be more difficult to save.[1]

This is where a true spiritual director becomes necessary. He or she breaks from the conventional wisdom of the day and approaches life by focusing on the will of God. Spiritual mentors identify the problems that lie under the surface of daily difficulties. James solves problems the world doesn't even recognize. The world is not particularly concerned with disappointment with God, disobedience to the Word of God or special treatment to someone who can do us a favor.

According to worldly wisdom, James is upset over the wrong things. Today's wisdom boils down to a short list of popular maxims: "If it feels good, do it." "No one can say what is true for someone else." "You have to look out for number one." "You only go around once in life, so you have to grab for all the gusto you can." "It's okay as long as you don't hurt anyone." Competition, self-advancement and personal autonomy comprise the wisdom of our day. The locus of authority lies in ourselves. James, on the other hand, argues that the true standard for self-evaluation lies not in ourselves, but in the revealed wisdom of God:

> If any of you lacks wisdom, he should ask God, who gives generously to all without finding fault, and it will be given to him. (1:5)

> The fear of the Lord is the beginning of wisdom,
>   and knowledge of the Holy One is understanding. (Prov 9:10)

> Where can wisdom be found?
> Where does understanding dwell?
> Man does not comprehend its worth. . . .
>   It cannot be bought with the finest gold. . . .
> "The fear of the Lord—that is wisdom,
>   and to shun evil is understanding." (Job 28:12-13, 15, 28)

> . . . Christ, in whom are hidden all the treasures of wisdom and knowledge. (Col 2:3).

> Oh, the depth of the riches of the wisdom and knowledge of God! How unsearchable his judgments, and his paths beyond tracing out! Who has known the mind of the Lord? Or who has been his counselor? (Rom 11:33-34)

The key to the wisdom commended by James is its dependence on the truth and character of God. From this source of wisdom every other quality draws its meaning. The wisdom of true spiritual direction is concrete and specific. The good life is sharply focused. It means persevering under trial without bitterness, obeying the perfect law that gives freedom, caring for orphans and widows in their distress, loving your neighbor as yourself, demonstrating faith in action. And it means doing all of these with an attitude of humility and meekness. The good life James had in mind encompassed a humble attitude and righteous action.

Internal Conflict

James diagnoses the hidden problems within in order to explain the obvious problems without. He identifies an internal source for sin and foolishness. He claims that the reason for bitterness, prejudice, useless faith and mouth damage can be found in one's heart. Religion reduced to presumption and performance must lay aside its pretense. It must be exposed for what it is.

Apparently James had in mind some professing believers who were similar to the pious people condemned by Asaph in Psalm 73: "Their mouths lay claim to heaven, and their tongues take possession of the earth" (v. 9). Jeremiah complained to God along the same lines; "You are always on their lips but far from their hearts" (12:2).

James gets right to the point. He does not accuse, but he warns emphatically: "If *you* harbor bitter envy and selfish ambition in your hearts, do not boast about it or deny the truth" (v. 14, my emphasis). No amount of orthodoxy can save people from the heart problem of bitter envy and selfish ambition. According to Peter Davids, "The problem is that zeal can easily become blind fanaticism, bitter strife, or a disguised form of rivalry and thus jealousy; the person sees himself as jealous for the truth, but God and others see the bitterness, rigidity, and personal pride which are far from the truth."[2]

James does not want believers to labor under a misconception. The wisdom these believers thought they had was not godly wisdom. It was inferior wisdom, pseudo-wisdom, devoid of the Spirit. Such wisdom presumes to speak for God but in fact is inspired by the devil. The shocking truth of this passage is not the contrast between worldly wisdom and heavenly wisdom, but the fact that professing Christians were in danger of substituting envy and ambition for true spirituality. They were confusing the Christian faith with their petty desires, personal opinions and selfish expectations. They were in danger of commending envy and selfish ambition as consistent with a Christian lifestyle.

The first step in dealing with demonic wisdom in the church, or anywhere else, is to identify it. But anyone who has had to deal with it knows how hard it can be to pinpoint it. Envy and ambition have a way of eluding detection. Airline passengers are screened and searched for concealed weapons before boarding, but church members can exude envy and ambition without setting off a warning alarm.

How can we be as confident as James in detecting evil and offering clear warnings? How can someone who is humble say that someone else is envious? How can someone who is peace-loving, considerate and submissive tell someone else that they are gratifying their own ego and denying the truth? We know it can be done because James did it. James the Just, the brother of our Lord, who demonstrated his peacemaking skills at the Jerusalem council (Acts 15), exposed envy and selfish ambition among professing believers. He "cared enough to confront." The wisdom of Christ required him to be honest and straightforward in his spiritual direction. Like Jesus before him, who laid bare the true motives of the Pharisees, James offered the painful diagnosis.

Wisdom's Résumé
James not only condemned the earthly and unspiritual wisdom of the devil, but he commended the wisdom of God. The best approach to problem-solving, James argues, is to expose the evil and internalize the good. There is a noticeable parallel between James's description of heavenly wisdom and Paul's description of the fruit of the Spirit in Galatians 5:22-26 and his description of love in 1 Corinthians 13.

Heavenly wisdom, living in the Spirit and agape love are variations on the same theme. All three view peacemaking as the Christian's high calling and the detection of sin a necessary part of spiritual direction.

Wisdom's résumé portrays a character of strength and sensitivity. The eight words used by James to describe wisdom present a fully integrated, multifaceted description of wisdom. The wisdom of God is first of all pure. Like the words and character of God, there is no mixed motive. Those who are wise take after God. Their ways are not devious and self-serving; they have no hidden agenda. Their behavior is not a façade to cover up self-serving attitudes and actions.

The wisdom of God is peace-loving. It does not stand up for one's rights. It does not look for trouble. Such wisdom does not use criticism to control people or situations. It does not hunt for a scapegoat to blame. Those who have such wisdom are not vindictive or combative or harsh. Not that they placate the wrongdoer or passively sit by when the rights of others are jeopardized. To be peace-loving is not to pretend everything is fine when it isn't. Peace-loving people pursue justice and righteousness.

The wisdom of God is considerate. It is gentle. It is tolerant and magnanimous. Such wisdom is eager to receive the stranger. It will never ignore the needy and tell them to fend for themselves. To be considerate does not mean giving people whatever they want whether it is good for them or not. A considerate parent gives a child what he or she needs to grow and mature. To be considerate is to be thoughtful in our concern for others. It involves saying and doing for others what we would appreciate for ourselves, especially for those without the means to reciprocate. Consideration must never fall prey to the false expectations of selfish people who confuse Christian service with customer service. We are not to be at the beck and call of spoiled Christians who have been waited upon for so long that they do not know how to serve.

The wisdom of God is submissive. It is persuadable, open to reason. Such wisdom is not stubborn and bullheaded, but it is faithful to the truth. It humbly receives the Word of truth. James reminds us that there ought to be a quality of mutual submission that pervades the household of faith. At the family level, parents, if they are not careful, can squelch true interaction with their children by dominating conversation. If every issue or question raised at the dinner table is met with an immediate, dogmatic response by the parent, the child will give up interacting. Children raised in such an atmosphere hardly know how to carry on a conversation because they are so used to conclusions and answers being drawn for them. Their thinking atrophies like a muscle immobilized in a cast.

A similar dynamic takes place in the church when true dialog is impossible because dominant personalities think they know all the answers. The submission encouraged by James allows a congregation to discuss the role of women in ministry or the place of the spiritual gifts—without division and hard feelings. The wisdom of God does not mean having all the answers and writing off those who disagree. To be submissive is to disagree agreeably. I remember many heated discussions around the dinner table when I was growing up that ended with the familiar saying, "We'll just have to agree to disagree." Submission involves distinguishing between primary convictions and secondary issues, and recognizing that mature Christians do disagree.

The wisdom of God is full of mercy, but in a world full of envy and strife the quality of mercy is strained. The need for mercy has not changed since Micah the prophet wrote, "What does the Lord require of you? To act justly and to love mercy and to walk humbly with your God" (Mic 6:8). We are naturally prone to excuse our own weaknesses while we hold other people accountable for theirs. We take credit for our good acts and deny responsibility for our bad. Instead of showing mercy, we inflate our own sense of well-being by belittling others, as the Pharisee in Jesus' parable looked down on the tax collector (Lk 18:9-14). Mercy is an effective tool in dealing with our self-serving bias. It helps us to redeem our inclination to put others down and raise ourselves up. It teaches us to bear with one another and forgive our grievances against each other. Mercy leads us not to condone or ignore evil behavior, but to forgive as the Lord forgave us (Col 3:13). As James said earlier, "Mercy triumphs over judgment!" (2:13).

The wisdom of God bears good fruit. Instead of short-lived special effects, wisdom produces an enduring harvest of righteousness. It doesn't leave a bad taste in our mouth the way bad faith does. True faith is fruitful. It nourishes the body of Christ with virtues that we can never have too much of—love, joy, peace, patience, kindness, goodness, faithfulness, gentleness and self-control (Gal 5:22-23). Such wisdom looks after orphans and widows in their distress and supplies the needs of the poor.

The wisdom of God is impartial, unprejudiced, nonpartisan. It is available to serve and befriend anyone in the name of Christ. Conventional wisdom thrives on giving to those who can return the favor. I know a businessman who intentionally caters to his wealthier clients. Since 20 per cent of his clients make up 80 per cent of his business, he gives his best customers special attention. He memorizes their children's names, sends personal notes and plans social gatherings. He may host a surprise birthday party at the country club and invite the client's banker, accountant and partners. This is how business operates, he claims. "You have to show you care. Besides that, it's profitable."

But he also feels this is how the church should run. The 20 per cent who give 80 per cent of the church's income should receive special attention. They need to be commended and made to feel important. They deserve a little stroking now and then so they will keep up the good work. I doubt that James would fall for this kind of reasoning. Instead, I can hear him advocating just the opposite—that those who deserve the most attention are those in need, as well as those who are open to spiritual direction.

The wisdom of God is sincere, devoid of hypocrisy or manipulation. True Christian commitment and affection prove, over time, to be both genuine and enduring. Christians can nurture lasting friendships because they are not masking their real feelings and concerns. The burden of going through the motions and meeting people's expectations is lifted. Pastors guided by this wisdom can be true spiritual directors rather than performers.

Some might think James does not fit his own description of true wisdom because he appears to be criticizing envy and selfish ambition on the part of his readers. But I believe his forthright approach to their needs and problems proves his sincerity, purity and impartiality. As a true spiritual director, he is neither apathetic nor domineering. He commends the wisdom that comes from heaven with authority and humility.

Seeds of Peace

Did James find that sowing seeds of peace conflicted with his work as a spiritual director? I do not think so. He knew it took hard work to cultivate the fruit of righteousness. He knew it required pruning the dead branches of sin as well as irrigating with living water. So often sowing seeds of peace requires sowing in tears. But James would probably concur with these words of the psalmist: "Those who sow in tears will reap with songs of joy. He who goes out weeping, carrying seed to sow, will return with songs of joy, carrying sheaves with him" (Ps 126:5-6).

What causes fights and quarrels among you? Don't they come from your desires that battle within you? You want something but don't get it. You kill and covet, but you cannot have what you want. You quarrel and fight. You do not have, because you do not ask God. When you ask, you do not receive, because you ask with wrong motives, that you may spend what you get on your pleasures.

You adulterous people, don't you know that friendship with the world is hatred toward God? Anyone who chooses to be a friend of the world becomes an enemy of God. Or do you think Scripture says without reason that the spirit he caused to live in us envies intensely? But he gives us more grace. . . .

Submit yourselves, then, to God. Resist the devil, and he will flee from you. Come near to God and he will come near to you. Wash your hands, you sinners, and purify your hearts, you double-minded. Grieve, mourn and wail. Change your laughter to mourning and your joy to gloom. Humble yourselves before the Lord, and he will lift you up.

Brothers, do not slander one another. Anyone who speaks against his brother or judges him speaks against the law and judges it. When you judge the law, you are not keeping it, but sitting in judgment on it. There is only one Lawgiver and Judge, the one who is able to save and destroy. But you—who are you to judge your neighbor?

JAMES 4:1-12

10

FROM
CONFLICT
TO
PEACE

JAMES follows up his positive description of peace-loving wisdom with a strongly worded rebuke. In the tradition of this ancient spiritual director, peacemaking hardly meant patching things up and smoothing over rough spots. James was not about to overlook sin in order to promote peace. As a true physician of the soul, he uses the convicting power of the prophet-pastor to remove the malignant malice from within the body of believers.

Peacemakers know two things: it is easier to tell people what they *want* to hear than what they *ought* to hear, and it is easier to speak the truth in anger than in love. Perhaps that is why James made sure to lay out the positive virtues of true wisdom before delving into the reasons for fights and quarrels. He does not flinch from administering painful truth, but his goal is positive, not negative. He makes every effort to keep the unity of the Spirit through the bond of peace (Eph 4:3).

A Sad Commentary

Life is hard enough as it is, so why do we make it harder? Why do we rob ourselves of the peace of Christ by fighting and quarreling? The very place intended to be a refuge has become a place of tension and conflict. This is especially sad because Jesus' chief strategy for evangelism was the love and justice lived out in biblical community. The key to evangelism for Jesus was not the individual believer but the body-life of the church. One reason we have chosen to explore other evangelistic strategies is that the "household of faith" has garnered such bad press. The infighting of Christians has driven a wedge between accepting Christ and belonging to the body of Christ. James's peace-making strategy reminds us of the words of Jesus:

> By this all people will know that you are my disciples if you love one another. (Jn 13:35)

> May they be brought to complete unity to let the world know that you sent me and have loved them even as you have loved me. (Jn 17:23)

James takes us below the surface to find the reason for the fighting and quarreling. His spiritual direction involves an inside look at the dynamics of conflict.

When the San Diego Yacht Club's sailboat won the America's Cup in 1988, the margin of victory was attributed to the ingenious design of the boat's hull. What mattered most in the race was below deck, not above. A better-designed hull enabled their sailboat to go faster.

Similarly, problems in the family and the church cannot be solved unless we look below the surface. It is easier to clean up external appearances than to change our motives and desires. Instead of fighting the battle within, we end up fighting one another. Larry Crabb in his book *Inside Out* identifies the problem:

> The hard-to-handle issues in our soul that keep us from relating to others deeply and constructively are ignored; and easier to handle

matters, such as social courtesies and appropriate language, become widely accepted barometers of spiritual health.

When this focus on measurable, superficial behavior serves to divert attention away from troubling realities within our soul, as it often does, then its effect is to help us cope by conforming our behavior to whatever standards we set. Change is largely external.[1]

The Battle Within

James uses strong language to describe the battle within. According to Alec Motyer, he "chooses the vocabulary of war to express controversies and quarrels, animosities and bad feeling among Christians, not because there is no other way of saying it, but because there is no other way of expressing the horror of it."[2] Where there ought to be peace there is war. Selfishly motivated discontent leads to fights and quarrels. James could not be more direct. Motyer explains: "He uses words indicative of extreme violence to expose the actual enormity of every dislocation of fellowship within the people of God: it is a declaration of war, an act of murder."[3]

The cause of this violence can be traced to evil desires battling within the hearts of believers. When Christians are not at peace with themselves, how can they be at peace with others? They are driven by impulses and ambitions that belong to the earthly, unspiritual and demonic wisdom described earlier. For James it is not an overstatement to call these professing Christians murderers. Jesus used similar language in the Sermon on the Mount: "You have heard that it was said to the people long ago, 'Do not murder, and anyone who murders will be subject to judgment.' But I tell you that anyone who is angry with his brother will be subject to judgment" (Mt 5:21-22).

Who can measure the devastating impact of broken relationships among Christians, and the resulting fallout from split churches? Who can gauge the anger seething below the surface of respectable Christianity? Who can estimate how much pain has been produced by disorder and disunity?

A faithful spiritual director reminds us of the dark motives and selfish pursuits that attack the body of believers. Numerous incidents in the Bible illustrate these evil passions and desires. Consider the ego-defending impulse of Cain when he killed his brother Abel (Gen 4). Angry with God for refusing to accept his offering, Cain took out his bitter rage on Abel. Cain was forewarned by God ("Sin is crouching at your door; it desires to have you, but you must master it"), but he refused to heed the warning. He gave free rein to his anger and turned unsuspecting Abel into a hated enemy, even though the problem was in his own heart and had nothing to do with Abel.

Absalom is another example of someone who sacrificed the harmony of God's people for the sake of his own ego. Intent on pursuing his personal agenda of power and success, he conspired against his father, David (2 Sam 15—18). He used his personal charisma to steal the hearts of the people so that he could steal the kingdom. Nothing stood in the way of his advancement, and as a result he put a whole nation through untold pain and suffering.

James reminds us that the same dynamics that produced a Cain and Absalom are wreaking havoc in the church today. True spiritual direction cannot ignore the dark urges and selfish motives fighting within the Christian community. The evil must be named. Peacemaking requires that the battle within be overcome, not overlooked.

Friendship with the World

There are choices of the heart that break God's heart. Spiritual directors help us to identify these choices clearly and resist them effectively. James contends that choosing friendship with the world is not an option. It is hatred toward God. The "world" James speaks of is best described by the apostle John:

> For everything in the world—the cravings of sinful man, the lust of his eyes and the boasting of what he has and does—comes not from the Father but from the world. (1 Jn 2:16)

Out of frustration and anger James cries, "You adulterers! How could you? You have done the unthinkable. You have scorned the love of God for selfish pleasure. The bride of Christ has violated herself, not through sexual immorality or heretical doctrine, but through envy, selfish ambition, and self indulgence."

God is the jilted lover, shunned as much by ordinary envy as by atheistic denial. James is God's advocate, offering spiritual direction where it is most unwanted: the hidden motives of the heart. "Don't you know," he exclaims, "that friendship with the world is hatred toward God?" His words sound a lot like the prophet Jeremiah: "You well-respected, cultural Christians have lived like pimps and prostitutes. You have had many lovers" (see Jer 3:1). The worldliness James condemns may not be as obvious as some sins, but it is just as real. John White says it well:

One can avoid dirty movies and beer parties and still harbor worldly bitterness and pride. We can be cigarette free, but untruthful, total abstainers, but gossipers, modest in dress, but acquisitive. . . . The heart of worldliness has more to do with carnality, possessiveness, jealousy, pursuit of beautiful material objects, pride, and snobbery than with the more traditional evangelical taboos. . . . The moral blindness which afflicts the church today is in part the result of church leaders . . . who condemn sins their hearers never commit while ignoring other sins that they and their congregations alike are guilty of.[4]

A short review of James's spiritual direction gives us some idea of the worldliness he is attacking. His readers were susceptible to "greeting-card Christianity." They had just the right words for the brother in need: "Go, I wish you well; keep warm and be well fed!" They favored personal opinion over biblical conviction and gave free rein to their point of view. They guarded self-interest and discriminated against the poor. They were hearers, not doers. They wanted a "decaffeinated Christianity," the kind that wouldn't keep them up nights worrying about widows and orphans.[5] They were good religious consumers and well-practiced critics of songs and sermons. They had a do-it-to-me attitude. Manage my fellowship. Meet my needs. They were members in good standing, but in danger of being God's enemies.

James is touching some raw nerves. He is putting into words what some of the believers undoubtedly felt but could not admit. They must have been stunned by his rebuke. Had their envy and ambition been so obvious? How did James see through their showroom piety?

God's opposition to our love affair with the world is a sign of his grace. Like a rejected lover, God does not let us go without a struggle. The bad news is that we have betrayed God. The good news is that God's grace will not let us go. But there is a way back to the wisdom that comes from heaven—the wisdom that is pure, peace-loving, considerate, submissive, full of mercy and good fruit, impartial and sincere. Before James calls for repentance he speaks of grace. He reminds believers that God goes before, convicting and empowering, longing for their repentance and restoration. God stands ready to forgive. God gives grace to the humble.

Internal Change
Spiritual direction offers no pat formula or easy technique to bring about a change of heart. Restoring our relationship with God can be likened to healing a marriage damaged by infidelity. Superficial changes cannot be substituted for the hard work of renouncing evil desires and seeking forgiveness. James commands a deliberate turning to God. Because God's grace goes before us, submission to God is a possibility.

James opens and closes his call to repentance with virtually synonymous words: "Submit yourselves, then, to God. . . . Humble yourselves before the Lord." Everything in between underscores a deliberate turning to God. Ten imperatives add up to a powerful challenge for believers: *submit* to God; *resist* the devil; *come near* to God; *wash* your hands; *purify* your hearts; *grieve, mourn* and *wail*; *change* your laughter to mourning; and *humble* yourselves before the Lord.

James's spiritual direction was intended to penetrate comfort zones and shake casual, compromising Christians from their apathy. In an age of entertainment, when nearly everyone wants to be upbeat and lighthearted, James calls for repentance. He challenges Christians to grieve, mourn and wail over their selfishness. "The sacrifices of God are a broken spirit; a broken and contrite heart, O God, you will not despise" (Ps 51:17). Peace begins with repentance.

True spiritual directors distinguish between genuine repentance and a guilt trip. Running ourselves down may be a way of avoiding personal responsibility, just as morbid self-disparagement can become a substitute for dealing with evil. The purpose of repentance is not to pull people down, but to turn people from sin. Remorse for our sin is not a sullen preoccupation with our failures, but a heartfelt sorrow for disobedience. God's grace disturbs and unsettles us, leading us to take responsibility for our actions and to turn to him for forgiveness. God's grace also informs and empowers us to do what is right.

The thrust of true repentance is essentially positive. We are not only commanded to draw near to God, but we are reassured that God will draw near to us. "Humble yourselves before the Lord, and he will lift you up" (v. 10) is a glorious promise. Repentance leads to transformation. Remorse gives way to joy. Not only does a love affair with the world cease, but the love of God is restored.

James insists that the evidence of repentance and humility is obvious. Offensive behavior ceases. The peace of God replaces human envy and strife. Shalom replaces slander, obedience overcomes a judgmental spirit and loving our neighbor fulfills the law of Christ. Those who are at peace with God will also be at peace with themselves. They will have no desire to slander or judge one another.

Our spiritual director's tough strategy for peacemaking works. James looks below the surface and diagnoses the hidden sins of envy and selfish ambition. His honesty overcomes our strategies of avoidance and deception. He emphasizes the consequences of our actions, and forcefully yet compassionately reminds us of the work of God's grace. His call to repentance cannot be misunderstood or easily ignored. Some friends may turn a blind eye to our sins, but a faithful spiritual director cannot. Others may make a lighthearted appeal to us to change our ways and clean up our act, but a prophet-pastor compels us to see the truth. Some will join us in a love affair with the world, but a true spiritual director will be bold and determined, willing to pay the price of true spiritual direction, even if it means losing our friendship. He not only has our best interests at heart, but he is also Christ's servant.

Now listen, you who say, "Today or tomorrow we
will go to this or that city, spend a year there, carry on
business and make money." Why, you do not even
know what will happen tomorrow. What is your life?
You are a mist that appears for a little while
and then vanishes. Instead, you ought to say, "If it is
the Lord's will, we will live and do this or that." As it
is, you boast and brag. All such boasting is evil.
Anyone, then, who knows the good he ought to do and
doesn't do it, sins.

JAMES 4:13-17

11

FROM
PRESUMPTION
TO
SUBMISSION

W HEN we want to know
how far it is to Chicago, we don't invent a new scale of measurement,
we use a standard measurement such as miles. This holds true for
spiritual direction as well. Instead of imposing on ourselves and others
our own standard of "making it" in the world, James encourages us to
submit to God's standard of living. Moving from presumption to
submission is not so much a problem of knowledge as a problem of
the will. The route is clearly marked, and the true spiritual director
consistently urges us to take it.

The Map of Spiritual Reality
"The great obstacle to discovering the shape of the earth, the
continents, and the ocean," Daniel Boorstin writes, "was not ignorance

but the illusion of knowledge."[1] Ancient mapmakers failed to distinguish between fact and speculation. They boldly drew what they *thought* was the shape of the earth. Imagine the difficulty this presented to early explorers. It wasn't clear where knowledge ended and imagination began. The mapmakers presumed to offer an explanation, but in fact only revealed their ignorance.

The temptation is strong in spiritual direction to speculate about the will of God just as the ancient mapmakers did about the shape of the earth. We can obscure the reality of God's will by shaping our lives according to our own dreams and expectations. Some Christians blend the will of God with worldly strategies of success. Others impose a legalistic code of conduct. In both extremes, presumption leads to confusion and heartache. Christians pursue courses of action they assume are compatible with the Christian life, but in fact are detrimental to their walk with God. What they thought was the will of God turns out to be a reflection of the American dream or a guilty religious conscience.

James reminds us that true spiritual direction rests on the known will of God. There is no need to make spiritual direction more complicated by refusing to do the obvious good. James knows that though we have decided to follow Jesus, we have a strong bias toward doing our own thing. We tend to impose our own will on the map of spiritual reality.

Ordinary Life

James packs a powerful one-two punch. Friendship with the world affects not only our relationships (4:11-12) but our decision making. The way we treat our neighbors and plan our lives demonstrates our values and reveals who we are. Good spiritual directors care about every aspect of our lives from friendship to business ethics. They focus our thinking on the spirituality of ordinary life: getting along with others, earning a living and thinking about the future. Spirituality not only pertains to the soul, but also to how we use time, expend energy, earn money, work out schedules. James teaches us that all these elements tie in with our devotion to God and with our understanding of his will.

Though some feel that James tackles church issues in scattershot fashion, I believe his argument flows logically in this chapter. If we sow the seeds of peace, we will reap the harvest of righteousness from the fields of relationships and work. Humility before God and peace with God has two practical consequences: First, we will give up slander and a judgmental spirit. We will replace the strategy of the world with true friendship. Instead of favoritism, self-interest, apathy and indifference, we will practice honesty, accountability, heartfelt concern and love. Second, we will change our priorities and the way we make our plans. Our vocational life, economic livelihood, educational pursuits and family vacations will be subject to God's direction and approval. There is no mystery in knowing what God expects. The challenge comes in following God's counsel.

Why does good advice need to be repeated over and over again, while bad advice takes hold with a mere suggestion? Why do children ignore a constant stream of wise counsel from their parents, only to leap at the mere mention of temptation? Our fallen human nature usually picks up on the bad and neglects the good, thus compelling spiritual directors to be persistent and patient. Ingratitude needs no instruction. Anger requires no encouragement. Selfishness demands no example.

It sounds so simple and straightforward. The will of God is not only clear, it is emphatic. We must not presume to judge a brother or sister. We have no business imposing our standard on others. Friendship with the world invariably results in distorting our understanding of others. Instead of seeing people from Christ's perspective we regard them from a worldly point of view (2 Cor 5:16). But friendship with the world also distorts our map of spiritual reality by affecting our planning and decision making. James warns against the impertinence of calling the shots. We must not presume on the basis of personal ability and profit motive to take charge of our lives and then invite God to give the blessing. If the law of God checks the presumption of a judgmental spirit, then the will of God challenges the presumption of a self-directed destiny.

Plan A

Friendship with the world follows a simple plan, so ordinary and commonly accepted that its danger is not readily apparent: "Today or tomorrow we will go to this or that city, spend a year there, carry on business and make money" (4:13). Parents typically strive to train their children to become self-motivated and self-sufficient. Their children's maturity is then evaluated on whether they take initiative, pursue a career, seize an opportunity and acquire a well-paying job. Most Americans have grown up on Plan A: good grades plus hard work plus a few lucky breaks equal success. Getting ahead and making a name for yourself is achieved through diligence and determination. After all, it sure beats the popular alternatives such as becoming a career student, a social dropout or a couch potato. In a sentence James has captured the spirit of the American dream. Behind this statement lie the high ideals of personal advancement, goal setting, strategic planning, self-initiative, upward social mobility and the profit motive. We can hear ourselves say something like it without a second thought. But our spiritual director James says, "Wait a minute—hold on. Have you listened to yourself lately?"

Friendship with the world is more deeply rooted in day-to-day living than we may realize. How we think about work and success may be influenced more by middle-class values, parental concerns, job expectations and professional goals than by the Word of God. The "professionalized" Christian is taught to play the game according to the rules. The playing field takes on a reality all of its own. The game controls how we think about the world; it determines our values and provides standards of success and satisfaction. When we are not playing the game, we are thinking about it. It absorbs, inspires and controls us. Our profession shapes the way we read people, orchestrates our lives and dictates how we measure time. In-group thinking conditions our self-worth and determines how we get ahead. Personal success relies on a social subculture which serves the interests of the marketplace. We live and move and have our being within our profession.[2]

It is easier to express this self-sufficient, self-important planning in the company of our peers than in a small group of serious Christians. Perhaps we are too conditioned to spiritualize our thinking among Christians and secularize our thinking among colleagues. Peer pressure influences us to reshape our map of spiritual reality. Friendship with the world dictates a different answer than we might give to a close Christian friend. Christian thinking is not sufficiently internalized to overcome the habits of secular thinking. We become conditioned to think of the real world as the university or the marketplace, and the church as an escape from the real world. The real world is the one in which, as singer Paul Simon puts it, "We work our jobs / Collect our pay / Believe we're gliding down the highway / When in fact we're slip slidin' away."

The Meaning Behind the Plan

Plan A covers all the bases. What else is there besides *time* ("today or tomorrow"), *purpose* ("we will go"), *place* ("to this or that city"), *goals* ("to carry on business") and *reward* ("make money")? Everything that matters is included. But James says, "Hold on, you don't even know what's happening tomorrow!" He then asks the one question that doesn't fit anyone's version of Plan A: "What is your life?"

When an experienced spiritual director cross-examines Plan A, several important things become clear. First, self-confident control is an illusion. It is presumptuous to dictate the course of our lives and predict the future. According to James, we have no business projecting our self-appointed destinies on our frail egos. Adult decision making has become childish boasting. We sound like kids playing make-believe, pretending to be whatever we choose to be. James dethrones the sovereign self. If we don't even know what is going to happen tomorrow, how can we talk so confidently about the future?

Second, the philosophy of life expressed in Plan A is seriously deficient. It answers the question "What is your life?" solely in material terms: life is money making, teaching courses, giving performances, selling real estate, climbing the corporate ladder, having a good time. If we follow Plan A, we will make great sacrifices for material gain, professional advancement and career success. We will orient our lives around the profit motive. We will pick up and move without another thought if it's good for business. We will believe that real living means picking the right career, knowing the right people, being in the right place at the right time to achieve success. Plan A shortchanges the meaning of life. It misses the essence of life. It means gaining the whole world and losing your soul. Riches can be arranged, but what a price!

Third, Plan A ignores the reality of death—at great spiritual peril. James challenges us to think of the brevity, not the predictability, of life. "You are a mist that appears for a little while and then vanishes" (4:14). If we play the role of the rich fool, we will pay for it—not in dollars and cents, but in broken families, empty lives, artificial piety. We may have bigger and better barns, but a time will come when we will be counting our losses. Plan A ignores the wisdom of David:

Show me, O Lord, my life's end and the number of my days; let me know how fleeting is my life. You have made my days a mere handbreadth; the span of my years is as nothing before you. Each man's life is but a breath. Man is a mere phantom as he goes to and fro: He bustles about, but only in vain; he heaps up wealth, not knowing who will get it. (Ps 39:4-6)

James gives us a big push toward reality. Preparing for death rather than ignoring it focuses our minds on God, our Creator and Redeemer; it looks at what is truly important in life. It helps us to say, with David: "Teach us to number our days aright, that we may gain a heart of wisdom" (Ps 90:12). James would be unimpressed with the way many Christians face illness and death. I know one man who has endeared himself to many over the years by visiting them when they were sick. But then one day, to his utter surprise, he was hospitalized with chest pains. "This wasn't supposed to happen to me!" he exclaimed. "I visit people in the hospital—I don't stay in the hospital." Of course, denial should not be confused with trust, nor naiveté with spirituality. But of all people, Christians should have an honest awareness of physical weakness and the brevity of life. True spiritual direction reminds us that life is short and preparing for death important.

Simply being around death does not necessarily impress us with the brevity and the spirituality of life. Sometimes those who live and work with death every day are the most materialistic and spiritually apathetic. They live in a material world and believe the old beer slogan that "you only go around once in life, so you grab for all the gusto you can." Instead of encouraging serious reflection, death can intensify the drive to pursue Plan A. True spiritual direction encourages us to understand death, not only as a hard fact of life, but as an awesome spiritual reality. Death is the harsh prelude to either a dreadful or joyful face-to-face meeting with the living God. James calls for us to change the way we look at life and death.

The one-word verdict on Plan A is *meaningless*. Undoubtedly James was well-versed in the logic of Ecclesiastes. He knew that failure follows futility and that despair follows disillusionment. Live for Plan A, James warns, and you are setting yourself up for a fall. "Meaningless! Meaningless!" says the spiritual director. "Utterly meaningless!" (Eccles 1:2). Give yourself to academics, business, pleasure, entertainment, and sooner or later you will find it is all for naught. "When I surveyed all that my hands had done and what I had toiled to achieve, everything was meaningless, a chasing after the wind; nothing was gained under the sun" (Eccles 2:11).

Plan B?
The alternative to compulsive overwork, executive egos, personal autonomy and money is not a second-rate Plan B. Rather it is the plan

of God, which James expresses as succinctly as Plan A: "Instead, you ought to say, 'If it is the Lord's will, we will live and do this or that' " (4:15).

The first problem in understanding this alternative is seeing it as an alternative. The pious hardly see any difference between Plan A and its opposite. What is James making such a big deal about? Hasn't he said all of this just to make sure we preface our actions with "if it is the Lord's will"? We have all met people who use "God's will" to get their way; "Lord willing" becomes a cliché used to rationalize selfishness. James is not talking about spiritualizing our decision-making. Anyone can say the words "if the Lord wills" and intend nothing more than to preserve religious decorum. Such pious talk only advertises our self-righteousness.

James is not looking for a change of words, but a change of heart. Parents who train their children to say "thank you" are more concerned about gratitude than etiquette. The customary phrase, however, helps to train the child's character so that the words eventually issue from the heart. James offers a simply statfed correction to a deeply ingrained philosophy of life. The big issue is between those who live—really live—as if God exists and those who do not.

The Known Will of God

The choices of the heart ought to be decided by following the revealed will of God. The advantages are not only practical, but eternal. Suffering leads to faithful perseverance. Evil desires within are resisted. The physical and spiritual needs of others are met. Justice is honored. Favoritism is rejected. Willfulness and vain opinion are checked. Slander ceases. Knowing God's will and obeying God's Word are one in the same.

The will of God that guides our decision-making is not left to our own subjective interpretation. It is not a mystery that God dangles before us like a carrot on a string. We need not proceed through life wondering whether we are in God's will or not. The fact of God's will is clear. As James understands it, the will of God is obedience to the commands of God. The difficulty with decision making lies not in our inability to predict the future, but in our willingness to obey. How we use our time, define our life, decide where we will live and what kind of work we will do is determined more by our life-pattern of obedience than by a fiery cloud or by Gideon's fleece.

The true alternative to the pride of Plan A is heartfelt obedience. We depend too heavily on personal impressions, inner urges and fuzzy feelings to justify dubious actions as God's will. There is an inherent conflict of interest in looking to our own feelings for direction when we should be following the straightforward counsel of God's Word. We need to take God at his word. Instead of leaning on our own understanding, which may be either too easy or too hard on us, we need to trust the Lord and obey. If we acknowledge God in all our ways, we can be confident of his direction (Prov 3:5-6). But if we disobey God's commands—no matter how much we talk about seeking God's will—we will not know his blessing.

James affirms the link between knowing the will of God and obeying the word of God in verse 17: "Anyone, then, who knows the good he ought to do and doesn't do it, sins." When it comes to God's will, we don't need to worry about what we don't know. We need to be concerned about what we *do* know. The debate is not over the future, but the present. We shut God out of our commercial life, our emotional life and our professional life if we refuse to apply his Word to these practical areas.

John Perkins writes: "One big problem I see, especially in young people who are enthusiastic about their faith, is that many ask, 'What is God's will for my life?' rather than thinking about God's will, period. I have people say to me, 'I want to know God's will for my life.' Then I find out that they have already decided what careers they are going to pursue, who they are going to marry, where they are going to live, how much they will earn in salary, how many children they will have and what kind of car they are going to buy. . . . It is not God's will that these people are looking for, it is their own will. They are not asking, 'What is God's program on earth and how do I fit in?' Their question is more like, 'How does God fit into my life?' "[3]

We cannot follow Plan A and simply merge into God's will whenever it is convenient. Spiritual direction confronts us with an either/or decision. Either we look for ways to serve or expect to be served; protect our self-interest or pursue justice; sow peace or raise rancor. The decision-making process depends on whether we are living for ourselves or taking up our cross and following Jesus.

The Bible offers a better concept of happiness. The blessing of God is given to those who walk in his ways (Ps 128). All of our concerns in Plan A will be taken care of if we seek first his kingdom and his righteousness (Mt 6:33). When we allow our minds to be renewed, we "will be able to test and approve what God's will is—his good, pleasing and perfect will," according to the apostle Paul (Rom 12:2). In so doing, "We not only let God be God as he really is, but we start doing the things for which he made us. We take a certain route; we follow certain directions; we do specified things. There are ethical standards to follow, there are moral values to foster, there are spiritual disciplines to practice, there is social justice to pursue, there are personal relationships to develop. None of it is difficult to understand," Eugene Peterson writes.[4] The obvious good is inviting, fulfilling and rewarding.

From James's perspective we are not losing much when we give up the pride of Plan A and submit to the plan of God. The choice is obvious. We accept the promise and live by faith. In the words of missionary martyr Jim Elliot, "He is no fool who gives what he cannot keep to gain what he cannot lose."

Now listen, you rich people, weep and wail because
of the misery that is coming upon you. Your wealth has
rotted, and moths have eaten your clothes. Your gold
and silver are corroded. Their corrosion will testify
against you and eat your flesh like fire. You have
hoarded wealth in the last days. Look! The wages you
failed to pay the workmen who mowed your fields are
crying out against you. The cries of the harvesters have
reached the ears of the Lord Almighty. You have lived
on earth in luxury and self-indulgence. You have
fattened yourselves in the day of slaughter.
You have condemned and murdered innocent men,
who were not opposing you.

JAMES 5:1-6

12
FROM
SELF-INTEREST
TO
SERVICE

P ROTECTING the church
from an invasion of demonic values is an important part of a spiritual
director's job. The task becomes more difficult when the invaders go
undetected by the Christian community. Like the ancient Trojan horse,
conventional wisdom is rolled into the center of the community,
looking more like a promising gift than a potential threat. The church
watches, feeling no fear of impending doom. Friendship with the world
is paraded as a new opportunity for success. The enemy is no longer
menacing, but inviting and appealing. The world's strategy for success
enters through the front door, disguised as a blessing. Its privileged
promoters—corporate raiders posing as benefactors—receive special
treatment as they milk the church of its spiritual and ethical vitality.

Ancient barbarians looked the part. Clad in animal skins and roving in packs, they savagely attacked and raped their prey. "Today's barbarians," Charles Colson writes, "wear pinstripes instead of animal skins and wield briefcases rather than spears."[1] They threaten the peace of the Christian community and the passion of the follower of Christ. They fatten their prey with public relations and appeal to the lusts of the flesh.

The Eye of a Needle

Money, sex and power are the benchmarks of the new barbarians. Beneath a veneer of charm, sophistication and claims of enlightenment lie the selfishness of the rich fool and the willfulness of the rich young ruler. Their barbarisms are numerous. They grind the face of the poor (Is 3:15) and trample on their heads (Amos 2:7). "They sell the righteous for silver, and the needy for a pair of sandals" (Amos 2:6). The wealth of the rich is based on the labor of the poor. The poor feed, clothe, educate, build and serve the wealthy. In return they are exploited and oppressed. The new barbarians crush the needy without a thought beyond their personal pleasure (Amos 4:1). They are consumers of a cheap, nonrenewable resource—the poor.

Against this deception our spiritual director raises his full fury. The church must not succumb to the barbaric values of the oppressor. The intensity of James's words reflects the reality of the threat. We do not know whether he was speaking directly to rich people in the church who claimed to be Christians, or whether he was denouncing those outside the church. Is his direct address—"Now listen, you rich people"—intended for his readers or staged for effect? The fact that he has already bluntly said, "You adulterous people, don't you know that friendship with the world is hatred toward God?" (4:4) suggests that James is aware of growing exploitation by the rich *within* the church.

We have already seen how rich people endangered Christian fellowship by expecting special treatment on one hand and denying their moral duty to serve on the other. James's illustration of dead faith refers specifically to those who have the means to meet the physical needs of others, but refuse to do so. Evidently, the toxic tenets of worldly success were seeping into the passions and ambitions of the church. James viewed the body of believers as under attack. His response is a lesson in spiritual direction and an encouragement to remain faithful.

There is today a popular deterrent to the prophetic intensity and spiritual direction of James. Christians don't like to get angry, especially with the wealthy and powerful. It is unfashionable to care so deeply about injustice, exploitation and oppression that we hold professing Christians accountable. We would sooner excuse the hypocrites and rationalize the excesses of the wicked. Who are we to criticize overconsumption and make people uncomfortable? After all, how people spend their money is between them and God. Extravagance is relative. One person's necessities are another's luxuries. It is easy to blur the difference between faith and denial, grace and selfishness, when Christian fellowship means accepting one another without regard to obedience.

James will not allow niceness to placate those who deserve to be warned, even condemned. The consequences are so dire that he will not allow himself to conceal his concern. His understanding of the difference between the way of faith and the ways of the world saves him from indifference. The intensity of his rebuke is not optional. His anger fits the crime.

The thrust of James's words recalls what Jesus said to the rich young ruler. "How hard it is for the rich to enter the kingdom of God! Indeed, it is easier for a camel to go through the eye of a needle than for a rich man to enter the kingdom of God" (Lk 18:24-25). The hyperbole underscores how hard it is for the wealthy to see beyond their material lives. They are possessed by their possessions. Their inflated egos, bloated schedules and customized lifestyles hinder them from seeing what is truly important and infinitely more valuable. Following Jesus becomes as difficult as getting through the eye of a needle.

Profits of Doom

James pronounces judgment. The rich are to weep and wail, not for what they have done, but for what will be done to them. The soul-destroying power of their wealth is as disgusting as spoiled fruit, sour milk, bad meat. Decaying, rotting wealth turns the stomach. Prized possessions are ready for the junk heap. Every material thing they trusted in gets trashed. Like maggot-infested manna, money becomes repulsive when it becomes the object of hope and security.

James's language of decay vividly depicts the ugliness of self-deception and pride fostered by confidence in material things. True spiritual direction causes us to face our vulnerability to the false security of money and success. Where we are tempted to see glamour, James sees garbage; where we see status, James sees depravity. The wealthy Laodicean church in Revelation 3 proudly boasted, "I am rich; I have acquired wealth and do not need a thing." But God's verdict was different. "You do not realize that you are wretched, pitiful, poor, blind and naked" (3:17). What appears enviable is instead a delusion that must be avoided. The deceit of wealth chokes one's understanding of God's Word (Mt 13:22) and turns the heart away from God.

Hoarded wealth is a spiritual carcinogen. It will "eat your flesh like fire," James warns, and it will "testify against you" (5:3). James agrees with the words of the Lord, "What is highly valued among men is detestable in God's sight" (Lk 16:15). For the spiritual health and vitality of the household of faith, James condemns the profits of doom.

Wall-Street Wisdom

James finds the world's prescription for profit guilty on three counts: "You have hoarded wealth in the last days. . . . You have lived on earth in luxury and self-indulgence. . . . You have condemned and murdered innocent men who were not opposing you" (5:3-6). We squirm under his pronouncement, wishing he had said "they" instead of "you." But his charge was probably leveled at those within the Christian community.

The issue? Concealed wealth versus shared wealth. The word "hoarding" is clearly perjorative, while "investment" is positive. James's practical spiritual direction raises a legitimate question: When do we cross the line between reasonable financial savings and greedy accumulation? The answer cannot be given in dollars, but in values. Only when kingdom values deflate dollar values will we be willing to exchange cash for compassion and security for justice. As it is now, too many Christians measure their worth, and the worth of others, in material terms.

According to James, hoarding stems from injustices in the marketplace. Wealth is derived by underpaying laborers for their work. Rich landowners conduct business according to the law of supply and demand without concern for a just wage. As long as they can find workers who will accept low wages, they do not have to pay more. And if the workers won't accept low pay, they don't have to work. James condemns such reasoning as evil and perverse. The "harvesters" have not been treated justly; instead of justice there is distress (Is 5:7). The gap between landowner and harvester is too great. The owner is forgetting that the land belongs to God. All means of production—from the factory to the farm, from Wall Street to the mall—belong to the Creator.

The huge salary inequality in the United States between farmers and brokers, teachers and physicians, nurses and professional athletes, laborers and executives points to injustice in our economic system. My boys were shocked to learn that I would have to work more than 100 years to earn the amount of money an NFL quarterback receives in one year. They were even more surprised when I said the president of the United States would have to work at least twenty years to equal the quarterback's annual salary. When supply and demand alone dictate wages, the value of a person decreases and the value of money rises. For James, the issue is justice, not charity. He is challenging the rich, not to give more, but to take less.

The parable of the rich fool captures the injustice James condemns.

Instead of sharing his good crop with his laborers and with those in need, the rich fool thinks only of himself. Confronted with success, he is as selfish as a two-year-old:

This is what I'll do. I will tear down my barns and build bigger ones, and there I will store all my grain and my goods. And I'll say to myself, "You have plenty of good things laid up for many years. Take life easy; eat, drink and be merry." (Lk 12:18-19)

The rich fool's hedonism leads to James's second grievance: conspicuous consumption. James draws some unattractive word pictures of the rich. They are like fatted cattle ready for the slaughter. They flaunt the symbols of success. Today's success ethic feeds on the notion that we have a moral duty to ourselves. The old self-denial ethic has been turned on its head, according to social analyst Daniel Yankelovich. "Instead of a concern with moral obligations to others pursued at the cost of personal desire, we have the concept of duty to self pursued at the cost of moral obligations to others. Personal desire achieves the status of an ethical norm."[2]

After James addresses the issues of hoarded wealth, conspicuous consumption and unjust wages, he makes a sober indictment: "You have condemned and murdered innocent men, who were not opposing you." Like the merchants of the great city described in Revelation who trade in the "bodies and souls of men," the rich disposed of people as they would any other commodity (Rev 18:13). James's charge may be referring to a legal proceeding of that day in which the rich used their power to crush the poor. Earlier he mentioned the rich dragging believers into court and slandering "the noble name of him to whom you belong" (2:6-7). The courts may have been used by the rich to protect their interests and condemn the poor. Then and now, the vested interests and political clout of the wealthy can bring great suffering upon the poor. Political decisions about toxic waste management, land development, gun control, gambling rights, health care and tobacco subsidies may favor well-financed lobbyists rather than the public good. The violence of the wicked may be couched in corporate maneuvers or legal proceedings, but it's as deadly as murder.

These rich people were apparently no different than the infamous Old Testament couple, Ahab and Jezebel, who destroyed Naboth to get his vineyard. A man of character, Naboth valued his land as a family trust. What would have been a trivial acquisition to King Ahab was Naboth's precious heritage. His refusal to sell testified to his wise stewardship: "The Lord forbid that I should give you the inheritance of my fathers" (1 Kings 21:3). The self-indulgent Ahab became sullen and angry. His dream of a beautiful garden on the plot of land adjoining his palace property was frustrated. He sulked and refused to eat.

But Jezebel had another idea. She understood worldly power and knew how to use it. Naboth's life meant nothing to her. "Is this how you act as king over Israel?" she asked her husband. "Get up and eat! Cheer up. I'll get you the vineyard of Naboth the Jezreelite" (1 Kings 21:7). So Jezebel plotted a hostile takeover. She wrote letters to Naboth's neighbors and associates and signed them in her husband's name. She wrote:

Proclaim a day of fasting and seat Naboth in a prominent place among the people. But seat two scoundrels opposite him and have them testify that he has cursed both God and the king. Then take him out and stone him to death. (1 Kings 21:9-10)

We have no idea whether Naboth's neighbors struggled with this evil assignment. We are simply told they did it. They accused Naboth of cursing the very God he honored. He was dragged outside the city gate and stoned to death, the helpless victim of cutthroat competition. He got in the way of Jezebel's power tactics. But the end of the story is not the death of Naboth, but the judgment of Ahab and Jezebel. The prophet Elijah was sent to condemn them to death for their evil (1 Kings 21:17-24).

In this powerful piece of spiritual direction, James forcefully challenges the body of Christ to be as honest about economic oppression and social injustice as the Bible is. He refuses to divorce spiritual matters from practical ones. If we do not hate what God hates, we do not love what God loves.

Patient Believers

James knows that believers live in a world where the wisdom of Wall Street prevails. He doesn't, however, let this fact of life soften his spiritual direction. His attack against social evil and oppression is blistering. But there is more to his direction than rebuke. He complements his harsh prophetic criticism with a pastoral strategy for living in a world where money is god. He neither mounts an activist campaign for a new economic order nor encourages plans for a utopian community. He calls for patience, not as a cop-out, but as we shall see, as an act of courage. Spiritual direction challenges believers to remain in the world without envy or bitterness. They must patiently endure injustice and oppression until the Lord comes, yet refuse to contribute to the evil. They must learn to see the Trojan horse for what it is and resist the temptation to become pinstriped barbarians.

Be patient, then, brothers, until the Lord's coming.
See how the farmer waits for the land to yield its
valuable crop and how patient he is for the autumn
and spring rains. You too, be patient and stand firm,
because the Lord's coming is near. Don't grumble
against each other, brothers, or you will be judged.
The Judge is standing at the door!

Brothers, as an example of patience in the face of
suffering, take the prophets who spoke in the name of
the Lord. As you know, we consider blessed those who
have persevered. You have heard of Job's perseverance
and have seen what the Lord finally brought about.
The Lord is full of compassion and mercy.
JAMES 5:7-11

13

FROM
PASSIVITY
TO
PATIENCE

AT FIRST glance our spiritual director's call for patience seems unreasonable. Who could listen to such a provocative and penetrating analysis of evil and remain patient? With all the abuse, discrimination and disdain going on, should the Christian merely take it on the chin and turn the other cheek? We might have expected something more proactive from James than a plea for patience.

Paper Tiger
After all the moral rhetoric, does the Christian's response to pinstriped barbarians amount to "grin and bear it"? Does James mean to spare us the emotional wear and tear of trying to overcome injustice? Is he a realist, accepting the fact that we can do little about evil but wait for

heaven? Does his rhetoric amount to nothing more than the roar of a paper tiger now tamed to the purr of a kitten? If that is all James has in mind, he certainly has no right to get us worked up against moral evil.

James has probably never served as anyone's model for patience. Instead of coming down so hard on the conduct of others, why didn't he lighten up and be a little more tolerant of human weakness? Instead, the entire thrust of his spiritual direction is unsettling and disturbing. He opposes double-mindedness and superficiality. He stirs us up against favoritism and discrimination. He challenges callous neglect and social injustice. He exposes worldliness with hard-hitting criticism. He accuses his readers of being "adulterous people" and condemns their boasting and bragging. From beginning to end, James attacks spiritual presumption in all its forms. Why then does he call for patience?

If we equate patience with being nice, politely tolerant and accepting, then James's call appears to be contradictory. That is why we need to understand the meaning of patience in James's spiritual direction. The word is not thrown in as an afterthought. Everything James has said moves us toward this exhortation. Like the apostle John writing from Patmos, James is our brother and companion "in the suffering and kingdom and patient endurance that are ours in Jesus" (Rev 1:9).

Wrong-headed Activism

James intends neither to inflame nor pacify his readers. His bold prophetic content is meant to convict, not enrage; to instruct, not incite. His analysis is honest and his direction straightforward. He does not want to mount a campaign, inspire a movement or lead a crusade. He entertains no grand illusion of changing the system, but has every intention of breaking the world's powerful hold on the community of faith.

Activism should never become a substitute for Christian thinking. Zeal without knowledge, no matter how well-intentioned, leads Christians astray. There are no quick fixes to social evil or to the evil within. We only frustrate ourselves when we feel we can change the world by marshaling public opinion, sponsoring an economic boycott or marching on Washington. Many evangelicals today are swayed by certain activists who distill Christian commitment down to a few issues. These activists then lead their "forces" against evil, hoping to capture media coverage and public attention.

Seldom do wrong-headed activists see eye to eye on abortion and apartheid, the justice system and the environment, big business and pollution, nationalism and feminism. The selective social agenda produces confusion and partisanship, reflecting a liberal or conservative platform rather than Christian ethics. The American church has substituted left- or right-wing political strategies for the patience James calls for. In the face of grave social injustices, many have neglected the meaning of Jesus' kingdom ethic.

Many of today's so-called Christian activists lack the understanding and resolve to endure patiently. The end product of easy-believism, religious individualism and fuzzy relationalism is a Christian whose patience is in short supply. When the whole counsel of God is neglected and the principle of the cross forgotten, bursts of wrong-headed activism are commonplace.

Stick-to-it-iveness

The purpose of patient endurance is to guard the Christian from either giving in to the world or attacking the world. Apathy and anger are both wrong. Complacency and conformity are as misguided as self-righteous resistance and rage. Regardless of the world's ridicule, persecution, manipulation and exploitation, the Christian must endure without succumbing to the mindset of the oppressor. The worst form of slavery occurs when the slave accepts the slave master's treatment as normal. Then the slave begins to think and act like his oppressor, eventually becoming one himself. The Christian is called to outlast the oppressor by faith.

"Be patient, brothers" is a holy challenge to stick to the principles of the gospel. Patience is not passivity. It has nothing to do with giving in to the evil powers that be. Waiting for heaven does not mean putting the struggle for justice on hold. Patience is the will to stay on course, to pursue righteousness in spite of evil and to persevere for the sake of Christ. It is a call to obey the whole counsel of God and to accept the Lordship of Jesus Christ, even when it looks like evil is winning. The key word here is *perseverance*, used by James in the first chapter:

> *Consider it pure joy, my brothers, whenever you face trials of many kinds, because you know that the testing of your faith develops perseverance. Perseverance must finish its work so that you may be mature and complete, not lacking anything.* (1:2-4)

Everything James has said is framed by the challenge to persevere. This is where he begins and ends his spiritual direction. Without patient endurance, a "long obedience in the same direction" is impossible.

The writer of Hebrews expressed a similar challenge:

> *Therefore, since we are surrounded by such a great cloud of witnesses, let us throw off everything that hinders and the sin that so easily entangles, and let us run with perseverance the race marked out for us.* (Heb 12:1)

Three illustrations of patient endurance stand out in James's mind: the hard-working farmer, the prophets and Job. Each example stresses two aspects of patience. First, patience demands intensity and passion, without a hint of apathy or passivity. This is not the way we usually think of patience. We tend to associate it with a calm, quiet demeanor. We assume patient people are laid back, easy to get along with, not uptight.

James's examples clearly show otherwise. The prophets were anything but quiet, passive observers. Instead, they were agitated, angry and aggressive. Jeremiah or Amos would never win awards for their gentleness. As a rule, God's "forth-tellers" went where they were not wanted, making statements no one felt like hearing. The last thing we would credit them with is patience; they were very impatient with disobedience. But James was not really speaking of a personality type. What he meant by patience was perseverance, endurance, spiritual tenacity, an unyielding conviction that will not give in to evil. The prophets could not be bought or compromised. They were not pacified or silenced.

Neither could Job, the man we traditionally call patient. He adamantly refused to submit to the wrong-headed perspective of his counselors. He would not let go of his understanding of righteousness. He would present his case before God if it were the last thing he did. From the prophets and Job we learn that to be patient does not mean to be nice; it means to be unyielding in our commitment to God.

The Work of Waiting

Second, patience requires the discipline of waiting upon God. "See how the farmer *waits* for the land to yield its valuable crop and how patient he is for the autumn and spring rains" (5:7). The built-in rhythm to farming parallels the Christian life. Farmers are dependent on a course of events beyond their control yet absolutely necessary for the growing process. The biblical idea of waiting involves our partnership with God. The harvest of righteousness does not grow out of our busyness or our individualism, but out of God's grace.

Hard-working farmers are never at a loss for things to do. They do not sit around twiddling their fingers, putting in time. They water. They weed. They fertilize. And as they wait for the crops to grow, they are not bored but expectant. This active form of waiting, this anticipation, sensitizes the farmer to the Creator's sun and land, rain and seasons. The fruit is not only a good harvest, but the farmer's heartfelt thanksgiving. Christians who wait trust in God's perspective and action. They realize that God's grace always goes before, preparing, providing and accomplishing. To wait for the Lord requires strength and courage. The psalmist encourages confidence:

Be still before the Lord and wait patiently for him; do not fret when men succeed in their ways, when they carry out their wicked schemes. (Ps 37:7)

Obedience is also called for: "Wait for the Lord and keep his way" (Ps 37:34). Rather than "lie in wait to shed blood," the righteous "watch in hope for the Lord" (Mic 7:2, 7). We may be tempted to meet force with force and accept the militancy of the oppressor, but those who wait on the Lord reject evil strategies. They are confident that God will hear "the cries of the harvesters." The work of waiting is filled with passion and hope.

James's spiritual direction is relevant for Christians fighting apartheid in South Africa or racism in the United States. It applies to believers in medical research who are expected to experiment with fetal tissue, or to those in law who are pressured to give up justice for expediency. Patience applies to Christians in business who are told to make career their number one priority. It speaks to high-school and college students who are tempted to give up their sexual purity. There is nothing heroic about this call to patient endurance: it is the common lot of pastors and widows, evangelists and teenagers, patients and professors. Perseverance in the truth and love of Christ is the high calling of each and every believer.

Body Language

The work of waiting and the passion of patience are put to the test daily in the attitude of each believer toward the body of Christ. The first signs of impatience are grumbling and complaining. When Christians carelessly speak against one another, their judgmental attitudes show that they have lost sight of Christ and his kingdom.

The use of the tongue has been a major concern for James. With the tongue Christians accuse God (1:13), express their anger (1:19), offer empty condolences (2:16), vainly boast about the future (4:13), and slander brothers in Christ (4:11). James impresses upon his readers the contradictory nature of this verbal abuse: "Out of the same mouth come praise and cursing. My brothers, this should not be" (3:10).

James understands that when believers are under pressure from external circumstances and from internal evil desires, they moan and groan against the people closest to them. They take out their frustrations on the church. We have all experienced this in our families. When we receive unfair treatment at work or suffer physical or emotional discomfort, most of us become more difficult to live with. We can become self-centered and expect the family to cater to our needs and compensate for our problems. When they don't come through for us—the way we think they should—we turn against them and make their life still more difficult.

All negative experiences such as difficult marriages, frustrated dreams, demotions at work, commotions at home, insomnia, high blood pressure, allergies, credit-card bills and insecurity can become fertile ground for fellow Christians to express discontent, even disdain, for each other. This happens for several reasons.

First, many mistakenly believe that the church exists only to meet their needs. They have a misguided and self-centered notion of the church. They expect more from the church than their brothers and sisters can possibly fulfill. Like a husband who expects his wife to meet his every desire, some Christians project unreasonable expectations on other Christians. They are like the Pharisees, who burdened others with impossible demands but never lifted a finger to help (Mt 23:4). Christians who think this way will always be dissatisfied, because the primary purpose of the church is not to meet their needs. It is to center our lives on Jesus Christ. Worshiping God and serving others come before our own needs.

Second, Christians may grumble more because of what I call the greenhouse effect. The climatic conditions in a greenhouse help everything grow faster, including weeds. In the church, as righteousness flourishes, so does self-righteousness. An atmosphere conducive to the fruit of the Spirit does not necessarily prevent the bad fruit of inflated egos, favoritism and empty piety from growing too. The church can fall into the trap of creating a positive climate for spiritual growth without giving attention to spiritual discipline and accountability. When this happens, people are never told they are wrong. Self-centeredness is never confronted. There is no supervision or mainte-nance of the church's growth. Complaints or attacks against fellow

Christians go unchecked. Dishonesty within the church grows until the orchard becomes a jungle.

Third, Christians take out their frustration on other Christians because they see the church as a scapegoat for their own disobedience and spiritual apathy. They are impatient with their own lack of spiritual growth and use the church as an easy excuse. It is too painful for them to take responsibility for their own immaturity. Instead of acknowledging their sin and receiving forgiveness, they grow bitter and critical. They complain that the church is never doing enough for children, young families, older adults, missions, evangelism or fellowship. They complain that there should be more tender loving care. They argue that if a small band of already overworked saints did more, then families wouldn't fall apart, teenagers wouldn't rebel, giving wouldn't be down, and the church wouldn't be so small. The "do-it-to-me" and "do-it-for-me" attitudes of many in the church causes believers to shy away from their responsibility to persevere. It is human nature to pin the blame for our problems on someone else. James knew that and warned believers to stop.

The Patience of God

Our spiritual director offers a simple incentive for keeping our words edifying: "The Judge is standing at the door!" (5:9). If we grumble against each other and impose our standard of expectation and perfection on others, we will be judged. The moment of reckoning is at hand. God will hold complainers and slanderers accountable for undermining the body life of the church. James's direction sounds like a mother telling her young child, "If you don't behave, you will be punished. Your father is due home any moment." The warning was meant to have a sobering and purifying effect. It was not meant to bully believers into submission, but to remind them of the consequences of their actions.

The apostle Paul similarly warned the Corinthians to watch what kind of church they were building on the foundation of Jesus Christ:

"If any man builds on this foundation using gold, silver, costly stones, wood, hay or straw, his work will be shown for what it is, because the Day will bring it to light. It will be revealed with fire, and the fire will test the quality of each man's work. If what he has built survives, he will receive his reward. If it is burned up, he will suffer loss; he himself will be saved, but only as one escaping through the flames" (1 Cor 3:12-15). Because of jealousy and quarreling, the Corinthians were building a shack on a foundation that was designed for a temple. Their body life was in shambles. Paul reminds us with the same seriousness as James that "we must all appear before the judgment seat of Christ, that each one may receive what is due him for the things done while in the body, whether good or bad" (2 Cor 5:10).

The underlying reason for spiritual reform and renewal, however, is not negative but positive. The goal of perseverance is not to dread judgment, but to earnestly expect the Lord's coming (5:7-8). Even though Christ's return is closer in our day than when James wrote his exhortation, it probably feels more remote to us than it felt to James. The passion of his patience and longing for Christ's return dwarfs that of most Christians today.

The fact that the Lord still has not come after two thousand years seems to jeopardize our sense of urgency. Our problem is that we have not understood the patience of God. The apostle Peter reminds us: "But do not forget this one thing, dear friends: With the Lord a day is like a thousand years, and a thousand years are like a day. The Lord is not slow in keeping his promise, as some understand slowness. He is patient with you, not wanting anyone to perish, but everyone to come to repentance" (2 Pet 3:8-9).

Perhaps we are in an even better position than James to measure the patient endurance of God. We are called to be patient, but we can rest assured that the greater patience belongs to God. God's timing is different than ours. The Lord of the universe is not limited to our time zone. Just as children have a different sense of time than adults, our understanding of time differs from God's. What looks like an embarrassing, unexplainable delay is only more evidence that the Lord is full of compassion and mercy. God is not procrastinating. The delay does not stem from divine indifference. "Important things are being done while we wait," Eugene Peterson writes. "The action on earth, seen from the heavenly place is a drama of victorious redemption."[1] James invites us to participate in the divine patience.

Above all, my brothers, do not swear—not by heaven or by earth or by anything else. Let your "Yes" be yes, and your "No," no, or you will be condemned.

Is any one of you in trouble? He should pray. Is anyone happy? Let him sing songs of praise. Is any one of you sick? He should call the elders of the church to pray over him and anoint him with oil in the name of the Lord. And the prayer offered in faith will make the sick person well; the Lord will raise him up. If he has sinned, he will be forgiven. Therefore confess your sins to each other and pray for each other so that you may be healed. The prayer of a righteous man is powerful and effective.

Elijah was a man just like us. He prayed earnestly that it would not rain, and it did not rain on the land for three and a half years. Again he prayed, and the heavens gave rain, and the earth produced its crops.
JAMES 5:12-18

14
FROM COMPLEXITY TO SIMPLICITY

COMPLICATED saints are Christians who are mixed up, pulled in one direction and then another. They are a bundle of narcissistic feelings and godly concerns. They have trouble sorting out favoritism from friendship, living faith from dead faith, worldly wisdom from heavenly wisdom. They vacillate between trust and anxiety, brotherly love and idle gossip, certainty about the future and reliance on God. One is never quite sure what complicated saints will do next. They are unstable in all their ways. For them, the Christian life is a series of ups and downs, highs and lows, moments of spiritual intensity and times of spiritual indifference. Discernment is forgotten in the distractions of life. James likened such believers to the churning sea, "blown and tossed by the wind."

Jonah is a great example of a complicated saint. The word of the Lord came to Jonah, telling him to "Go to the great city of Nineveh and preach against it" (Jon 1:2), and Jonah headed in the opposite direction. He wanted nothing to do with the pagans living in the capital of Assyria. After endangering others' lives, causing much commotion and disobeying God outright, he came to his senses in the belly of a fish. God gave him a second chance, and this time Jonah obeyed. He preached a message of judgment: "Forty more days and Nineveh will be overturned" (Jon 3:4). He issued that message courageously and emphatically from one end of the city to the other.

But Jonah was filled with confusion. He was a mix of prophetic discernment and ethnic prejudice. He proclaimed the Word of God, yet cherished his own pride. He preached judgment and repentance, but refused to pray for Nineveh's repentance. Nevertheless, the king of Nineveh had ears to hear Jonah's message from God. He publicly repented in sackcloth and ashes, and called for the entire city to fast and confess its sins.

Few prophets have witnessed such dramatic conversion on such a large scale. But Jonah, we are told, was displeased and angry. He should have been overjoyed, but instead he regretted ever having come to Nineveh. He was so despondent he wanted to die. He found a comfortable seat east of the city, hoping to see the fireworks. As he waited under the hot sun, a fast-growing vine provided shade. But the next morning the vine had withered. And nothing had happened to the city. The sun blazed down on Jonah's head, and he was filled with anger—at the Ninevites, at God and at the withered vine. He wanted to die.

God chose not to placate Jonah but to exasperate him. He caused the leafy vine to grow and give Jonah shade, only to send a worm to destroy it. He provided the scorching wind and hot sun to play with Jonah's complicated emotions. And at that moment, Jonah cared more about the vine than the great city of Nineveh and its 120,000 people. So God said to Jonah (4:9), "Do you have a right to be angry about the vine?" And Jonah responded, "I do!"

Complicated saints nurse wounded pride, slander others and seek to impose their own will on God. They make the Christian life unnecessarily difficult and traumatic. Many of us, like Jonah, find it hard to move from mixed motives to pure motives, from a divided heart to an educated heart. God must send whales and worms to get our attention. The confusion is of our own making. Jonah's escapade makes for a great drama, but it was totally uncalled for. It was needless trauma.

When James offers his direction, he is writing to some New Testament Jonahs who insist on being complicated saints. They are so deeply attached to their pride and prejudice that they have unwittingly made it a part of their Christian religion. They actually feel holy when they are doing something evil.

Racial prejudice is one of those deeply rooted sins that, if not extracted, endangers the whole Christian life. I recall the difficulty Gene Paisley, a Canadian farmer, had when his only daughter, Brenda, fell in love with David Mensah, a black African from Ghana. Gene had first met David, a Bible college student, when David spoke in Gene's small country church. He was moved by David's genuineness and their friendship began to grow. He invited David to work on his farm one summer. They learned they had a lot in common. They loved Christ and they loved the land. It was a beautiful thing to see: a lean, wiry, very black African who had competed internationally in track, working alongside a big, hearty, ruddy-faced Canadian dairy farmer. They talked a lot about crops, cows and the Great Commission. Gene was profoundly impressed with David's spiritual maturity and his ability to share Christ with others. But he also noticed that his daughter, Brenda, and David were growing closer and closer as friends.

It was the last thing in the world either David or Brenda had expected, but their friendship, over time, matured into love. They began to talk of marriage—something Gene had not bargained for. It went against his cultural sense of what was right and proper. He didn't like it, but didn't know quite how to oppose it. He had already accepted David as a close Christian brother.

As time went on, Gene became convicted about his attitude. He and his wife, Laura, talked and prayed and struggled with the realization that they had no Christian reason for objecting to David as Brenda's husband. After several more months, Gene's view shifted even further. Rather than oppose or reluctantly accept David as his future son-in-law, he decided to give his wholehearted approval to the marriage. And to show his unconditional acceptance, he even traveled to David's remote village in Ghana to meet David's father and to express the honor he felt in receiving David into his family. Gene is a powerful testimony to the power of love over prejudice. Mixed feelings and motives were overcome. Strained relationships gave way to peace and joy. Discernment mastered discrimination.

Simple Honesty

When James offered his spiritual direction about swearing (5:12), he was confronting a long tradition of elaborate rules for giving your word and taking vows. If, for example, you used the name of God in your vow, then you were bound to fulfill your word; but if you did not include the divine name you were permitted to renege on your promise.

Jesus addressed this subtle form of religiously approved deception in the Sermon on the Mount. His main concern was not profanity, but perjury. He argued that the precise wording of a vow-formula is irrelevant. The issue is integrity: whether the name of God is mentioned does not affect one's obligation to keep his word. Neither Jesus nor James were talking about official vows taken in a court of law; instead, they were concerned with ordinary, everyday honesty. They wanted to make it clear that there is no such thing as making a particular commitment "more honest" by invoking a vow. A person's yes or no should be completely honest. According to John R. W. Stott, both Jesus and James emphasized that honest people "do not need to resort to oaths; it was not that they should refuse to take an oath if required by some external authority to do so."[1]

The issue of telling the truth is still a big problem. Today's complication has less to do with the wording of oaths and vows and more to do with intentional deception. We have come to expect it, especially from public personalities. To almost any question or issue, there is an "official" side and an "off the record" side to telling the truth. Much of our public communication is a performance. The real world—the truth—is behind the scenes.

In the PBS special "The Truth about Lying," Bill Moyers reported that the seven astronauts who died in the Challenger space shuttle disaster were never told of the dangers of launching in cold temperatures. A behind-the-scenes debate raged between the engineers of Morton Thiokol on one side and the company's managers and NASA on the other. To bolster NASA's public image, information about the dangers of the launch was suppressed. When Morton Thiokol's engineers refused to give the go-ahead, they were removed from the decision-making process. In spite of their serious objections, the Challenger was launched and millions witnessed the disastrous consequences. Once the private debate became public, the world learned of NASA's deception and cover-up.

Public communication, Moyers says, has become the art of deception. President Lyndon Johnson deceived the American people on the true nature of the conflict in Vietnam. He refused to tell America the cost of mobilizing our armed forces out of fear that his plans for "the Great Society" would be jeopardized. Congress and the American people did not learn the truth about Watergate and the Iran-contra affair until layers upon layers of deception had been scraped away. Intentional deception is now commonplace in political communication. Truth is carefully selected and filtered to convey to the public what politicians want the public to think. Truth is no longer simply told; it is "managed."

What is true in politics is also true in business. There is a visible network of people with official, authorized information, and an underground network of those who know how things really are. Marketplace savvy usually means that people know how to work the truth to their own advantage. No one ever says exactly what they mean. An implied yes one day can be easily switched to a no the next if it serves self-interest. The result is a tangled net of communication fed by misleading affirmations, innuendos, well-placed rumors, technical jargon, vague statements and controlled information.

Those in Christian ministry can also give a self-serving slant to the truth. There are often two sides to a missionary's report or an evangelist's fund-raising letter. Sadly, many in "ministry" present a carefully monitored report of what they want the Christian public to know. We have grown so accustomed to managing information and presenting an appealing image that we hesitate to be honest about our reservations, disappointments and concerns. Is our major concern to get the truth out or to worry about how people will receive it?

If we take James's spiritual direction seriously, we will want our yes to be a *true* yes, whether we are speaking publicly or privately. We will not say something to someone's face and something else behind their back. We will not look for loopholes and excuses to evade the truth. We will not say what people want to hear in order to create a positive impression.

In contrast to deception, integrity is very simple, though not always easy or expedient. It treats everyone alike. A conversation with a child deserves the same truthfulness as a conversation with God. Truth fosters trust and nurtures confidence. Most importantly, integrity honors the God of all truth and exposes Satan, the author of deception.

Simple honesty has two sides, the positive and the negative. We cannot say yes to some things without saying no to other things. We say amen to the gospel of Jesus Christ and no to sin and evil.

The complicated saint makes bold statements to the Lord, such as "I will follow you wherever you go" (Lk 9:57), without counting the cost of commitment. His easy yes to God, said in a moment of excitement, reflects more of a passing fancy than a settled conviction. Revved-up emotions may be great for filling out response cards, but careful consideration and serious reflection are necessary for a lasting affirmation of God's will. Jesus knew full well that a yes without understanding would probably turn into a no. Jesus also found a "yes, but" unacceptable, as in, "I will follow you, Lord; but first let me go back and say goodbye to my family" (Lk 9:61). We cannot qualify our affirmation to God with stipulations to guard our self-interests and preferences. "No one who puts his hand to the plow and looks back is fit for service in the kingdom of God," Jesus said (Lk 9:62).

The heartfelt affirmation of Christian worship and the well-informed, decisive yes of Christian commitment leads to an equally resolute no. The grace of God "teaches us to say 'No' to ungodliness and worldly passions, and to live self-controlled, upright and godly lives in this present age, while we wait for the blessed hope—the glorious appearing of our great God and Savior, Jesus Christ" (Tit 2:11-13).

This is the yes and no of discernment and wisdom, rather than the self-righteous yes and judgmental no of a legalistic attitude. Uncomplicated believers reflect the wisdom of God in words designed to communicate a true yes and a true no. They say what they mean to say. They tell it like it is. They are as good as their word.

Simple Imperatives

I believe that we have made James's next words of direction (5:13-18) much more complicated than he intended. The complications result by missing the obvious point of James's closing summary. As a spiritual director, he guides believers in the basics of spiritual formation. Christians need to be attentive to the importance of prayer, praise, confession and the power of God to heal and restore. Spirituality does not involve a complex, elaborate response to the ups and downs of life. There are no secret techniques and self-appointed gurus. We do not need special speakers and seminars as much as we need faithfulness.

James asks short, direct questions: "Is anyone in trouble?" "Is anyone happy?" "Is anyone sick?" These are not hard to understand nor hard to answer. If you are under pressure from difficult circumstances, then pray. Don't lash out or hold it in. And whatever you do, don't turn away from God. Turn *toward* him. If things are going well, then take care not to forget God. You should sing and praise God. In all situations, good or bad, remember God. James's words call to mind the apostle Paul's spiritual direction:

Speak to one another with psalms, hymns and spiritual songs. Sing and make music in your heart to the Lord, always giving thanks to God the Father for everything, in the name of our Lord Jesus Christ. (Eph 5:19- 20)

Two Extremes

Most of the confusion that surrounds this text comes with James's third question and his answer: "Is any one of you sick? He should call the elders of the church to pray over him and anoint him with oil in the name of the Lord. And the prayer offered in faith will make the sick person well; the Lord will raise him up" (5:14-15). Ironically, some Christians have used this text to teach healing on demand, while others have used it to defend the practice of anointing the dying as a last rite. Both views are extreme.

The first extreme treats James's spiritual direction as a manual for healing. If you obey the prescribed procedure and add faith, a miraculous healing will result. But this view overlooks several important truths which James has already offered. From the outset, he has prepared believers for facing "trials of many kinds." He is convinced that the testing of one's faith, which leads to perseverance and wisdom, is more important than perfect health.

Furthermore, James has emphasized how practical true spirituality is. True religion is not above sickness, death, grief and loneliness. If oil and prayer meant instant healing, there would be little need to provide meaningful service to orphans and widows. The test of authenticity, according to James, is not whether the dying are healed through our ministry, but whether the grieving are cared for through our service.

James has stressed faith and action to such an extent that we should never misconstrue "the prayer of faith" as a substitute for meeting the medical, material and emotional needs of others. Nor should we pray for healing without remembering James's admonition against misguided, selfish prayers: "When you ask, you do not receive, because you ask with wrong motives, that you may spend what you get on your pleasures" (4:3). The confidence James had in God's power to heal ought to be understood in light of his emphasis on the brevity of life: "What is your life? You are a mist that appears for a little while and then vanishes" (4:14). If true spiritual direction prepares us for a temporary earthly pilgrimage full of struggles, we can hardly expect healing on demand. James encourages believers to live in the tension between the already and the not yet: "Be patient, then, brothers, until the Lord's coming" (5:7). Instead of promising perfect health, he calls for perseverance. He is confident that nothing, including disease and death, can separate us from the love of Christ.

The other extreme view of this text is the Roman Catholic practice of last rites, or "extreme unction," which developed in the medieval Roman church. Support for the rite was linked to this verse in James. The priest anointed the gravely ill person, in preparation for death, as an act of spiritual healing to remove all sin. For centuries this anointing was delayed until the very last moment of life, to assure that the dying person had no opportunity to sin before death. The purpose of the rite was to make a person more acceptable to God after death.

In contrast to ancient and modern interpretations, James's intention was very simple. The seriously ill believer who was unable to go to the elders should request the elders to come and pray over him or her. The anointing with oil may have been intended as an outward sign of the inward power of prayer (Mk 6:13) or offered medicinally for its soothing effect (Lk 10:34).

There is no magical power to this oil. Nor is there any suggestion that only oil "consecrated" by a priest or a bishop is acceptable. There is no hint that this ministry to the sick belongs to someone who claims to have the gift of healing. Nor is there any implicit exhortation that the church should sponsor public healing services.

As we have already seen, James encourages the church to meet the physical needs of others. If people become gravely ill, James advises them to consult the leadership of the household of faith. It is a sign of faith and dependence upon God for Christians to do this. The initiative lies with the individual believers; it is not imposed on them. Even the gravely ill contribute to the body life of the church by requesting prayers of faith empowered by the name of the Lord. The physical side of spirituality is not depreciated. Once again we are reminded that we are neither bodies without souls nor souls without bodies, but bodies *and* souls in community.[2]

James expects physical, emotional and spiritual healing to take place among God's people who pray in faith. Prayer does not impose our will on God's will. Jesus taught that the essence of prayer is "not my will, but yours be done" (Lk 22:42). Health is a gift from God that we can ill afford either to secularize or spiritualize. The power of healing lies neither in "consecrated" oil and the laying of hands nor in the god of biomedical technology.

The Bible establishes some kind of link between physical health and righteous living. It does not say that ill health automatically derives from personal sin. But we live in a fallen, broken, sin-filled world, and suffer in our bodies and minds the effects of that environment. And sin can have physical consequences. "Sexual immorality, impurity and debauchery; idolatry and witchcraft; hatred, discord, jealousy, fits of rage, selfish ambition, dissensions, factions and envy; drunkenness, orgies, and the like" (Gal 5:19-21)—the consequences of these sins can be felt physically and spiritually. They destroy body and soul. Ultimately, the best remedy for physical illness stemming from these spiritual ills is not penicillin or valium, but repentance and confession.

Perhaps these two extremes, healing on demand and extreme unction, help to clarify James's simple teaching that only prayer and praise, confession and faith, will lead to healing, forgiveness and endurance. The power of the Christian life and the effectiveness of the community of faith rest in the living God, who hears and answers the prayers of those who earnestly seek him.

An Uncomplicated Believer

James draws his spiritual direction to a close with an unlikely example: the powerful figure of Elijah. We have an intuitive sense that biblical characters are out of our league. They are stars in the NBA or NFL of spirituality, and we are still in little league. But according to James, "Elijah was a man just like us" (5:17), a simple, uncomplicated believer who followed God and prayed to him in faith. It was Elijah who took on the wicked king Ahab and the prophets of Baal. He prayed fervently that the rain would cease and it did. God sent a drought as judgment against the idolatry and wickedness of Israel. It was not that Elijah prayed with superhuman intensity or in a special manner. Alec Motyer explains what James meant: "The Greek says, literally, 'with prayer he prayed' and the meaning is not his fervency, nor even his frequency of prayer, but that 'he just prayed'—that, and nothing more!"[3]

The point of James's spiritual direction is that the ordinary Christian is to be like Elijah—faithful in prayer, strong in character, obedient to the Word of God. We do not have to work our way up a spiritual hierarchy of sainthood. There is no complicated formula for successful prayer and spiritual strength. James offers a welcome alternative. Prayerful dependence upon God is the simple yet crucial way of facing the daily grind as well as the times of joy. There are many complex ways we can distort and mystify spiritual direction. Life is filled with complicated saints like Jonah who muddle the Christian life with petty grievances, cultural conformity and self-indulgence. The task of a good spiritual director is to encourage us with positive examples such as Elijah, a simple, confident, uncomplicated servant of God who prayed in faith and witnessed the power of God.

My brothers, if one of you should wander
from the truth and someone should bring him back,
remember this: Whoever turns a sinner from the
error of his way will save him from death and cover
over a multitude of sins.

JAMES 5:19-20

15

FROM
GRAND
DESIGNS
TO
BASIC
COMMITMENTS

J AMES wraps up his spiritual
direction by sharing his purpose for writing: to help brothers and
sisters in Christ come out on top in the spiritual struggle. Instead of
advertising his efforts up-front—the temptation many fall into today—
James concludes with a simple, self-effacing explanation. His basic
description of spiritual direction is postponed until the very end. Like
an artist who interprets his finished work, James offers a perspective
on why he has written. And his purpose should be shared by all who
serve as spiritual directors—parents, pastors, teachers and friends.

A Purpose Statement
When James refers to "someone" who seeks to restore a wayward
brother or sister, he is first thinking of himself. This is the work that

he has patiently and passionately sought to fulfill. His whole letter has been directed to those who are tempted to wander from the truth.

From beginning to end, his letter has been a work of spiritual direction devoid of ego-gratifying self-expression. James has been a prophet-pastor to spiritual refugees who wrestle with disappointment with God, friendship with the world and submission to the Word of God. He is not patting himself on the back by summarizing his own efforts on their behalf. He is rather commending the work of spiritual direction, first for their own benefit, and then for others'. The reminder he now gives has been on his mind from the outset. He is fully aware of how much is at stake in how they receive his spiritual direction.

His closing statement sounds like something out of Proverbs. What he has sought to do never goes out of style. Spiritual direction has universal significance and enduring relevance. James succinctly summarizes the main task of the household of faith, the Christian home, and pastoral ministry: the obvious yet difficult work of helping people turn away from evil and turn to God. This job description applies to every believer. We never rise above this high calling, nor can we ever afford to leave this work to others. James wants to impress us with the necessity of back-to-basics spiritual direction. If we are not fulfilling this purpose in our churches and homes we are disobeying both the Great Commission—"Go and make disciples . . . teaching them to obey everything I have commanded you" (Mt 28:19-20)—and the Great Commandment—"Love the Lord your God . . . and your neighbor as yourself" (Mk 12:30-31). Amid all the hoopla over what is expected of Christians, we may have missed this basic truth.

Holy Crusades

There is something to be learned by comparing the way James expressed the purpose of his ministry and the way Christian organizations and pastors promote their agendas. His purpose statement is so unlike what we have come to expect from religious promotional appeals that we may be tempted to minimize or even ignore its importance.

All sorts of people are trying to impress us with what they want to accomplish in the name of Christ. "Christian" advertising has come of age, with global projects and all-out campaigns for megabucks. Reaching a hundred million souls for Christ depends upon "my" financial response to their flashy direct-mail campaign. A new multimillion-dollar family life center designed to enhance Christian fellowship needs "my" support today. Photos of starving children are juxtaposed with photos of evangelical Taj Mahals.

Today's holy crusade bombards the innocent Christian with grand designs and elaborate schemes, all for the sake of selling holy purposes. We are so enamored with large-scale efforts and heroic activities that we overlook the simple purposes of God. The work of spiritual direction is lost in the hype.

James's humility rebukes this self-promotion by Christian organizations. The kingdom James serves is the kingdom of God, not the corporate kingdoms of humanity. He seeks the righteousness of Christ, not favorable publicity. The truth he holds so dear is not the quarterly report but the Word of God. He does not have to sell us on what he seeks to do; he has already done it. By the time he expresses his purpose statement, the truth of his spiritual direction has gone before.

Most people who offer me true spiritual direction are not even immediately aware that they are doing so. They do not come to me advertising their efforts. My wife, Ginny, has probably never thought of herself as my spiritual director, but she is constantly concerned that I not wander from the truth. I cannot begin to count the ways that she has unobtrusively yet directly helped me turn from sin. She has been like James to me—working to preserve and deepen my commitment to Christ and to the household of faith.

Managing Felt Needs

There is a significant difference between James's approach to pastoral ministry and that of many pastors. James's focus is on the spiritual welfare of his brothers and sisters in Christ. He is singularly committed to the task of directing people to God. The modern people-pleasing pastor, caught up in a whirlwind of religious duties and activities, hardly finds time for the kind of work prescribed by James. Spiritual direction enters the picture as an afterthought. Pastors are not expected to assume the spiritual authority exercised by James, nor do they usually feel the freedom and responsibility to serve as spiritual mentors.

Sadly, many of the relational and organizational qualities looked for in a pastor have more to do with running an institution than offering spiritual direction. Too often pastors are expected to be program coordinators, therapists, public relations experts and fundraisers rather than spiritual directors. Faithfulness to the gospel ranks below people feeling good about themselves. Increased giving is a surer sign of church success than spiritual growth. The excitement and activity of a new church building generates renewed enthusiasm among Christians unaware of the spiritual disciplines. Unlike the teaching of James, much of today's preaching is either repetitious or entertaining, serving more to distract than to direct. The great truths of God's Word are squeezed into suburban tales of pastoral self-expression, packaged neatly in predictable and pleasing sermons. Centuries of Spirit-guided theology and the great adventure of the Spirit's movement in history are set aside in favor of an "extra-lite" diet of fast-food faith.

Vision Versus Revelation

A true spiritual director reminds me of an old-fashioned farmer. Farming knows a rhythmic pattern of activity, season after season. The land is plowed, the seed planted, the crops irrigated and cultivated. The farmer works and waits. He participates in nature's rhythm, depending on a balance of sunshine and rain to grow his crops. He is a coworker in nature's pattern of growth and fruitfulness. He participates in the whole process, from tilling the ground to bringing the harvest to market.

Spiritual directors are like farmers who love the land and understand their work. They are not fast-driving entrepreneurs running from this venture to that project. They work in tandem with God to cultivate faithfulness and obedience. They don't strive for success in terms of numerical goals or impressive deals. They work day after day in obedience to the Word of God. There is a rhythm to spiritual direction, a rhythm of prayer and patience, encouragement and admonition.

The difficulty with spiritual direction is that many Christians find the work boring. They want to see things happen overnight. They want God to work quickly and decisively. They are more inclined to count the number of souls being saved than to provide genuine friendship to needy brothers and sisters. They want a feeling that they are part of something big. Surrounded by inspirational leaders and religious excitement, they are constantly reassured that they made the right decision in becoming a Christian. But little is said about becoming like Jesus.

Such Christians want pastors and churches with "vision." They want measurable goals and tangible objectives. They quote the well-known proverb, "Where there is no vision the people perish," without realizing the fundamental meaning of the biblical vision. They fail to discern that their philosophy of ministry and style of Christian living is more American than it is biblical. They misinterpret the course of spiritual direction. The hype surrounding their "vision" detracts from the well-defined truth and holiness of the biblical vision. The proverb correctly reads, "Where there is no revelation, the people cast off restraint; but blessed is he who keeps the law" (Prov 29:18). The cure for lifeless Christianity is not found in growing numbers, spectacular sanctuaries, charismatic leaders or lively singing. Nor is it experienced in small, intimate groups of Christians who cater to each other's felt needs. True spiritual vitality depends, as it always has, on faithfulness and obedience to the Word of God in the ordinary, daily tasks of life.

The gospel the world needs to see and hear sets people free from evil desires, instability, selfish biases and greed. This is not a promotional evangelism that sells cheap grace, but a prophetic evangelism that offers costly grace. It is the evangelism of everyday faithfulness to the perfect law of liberty, the evangelism of Jesus and the apostles, the evangelism that really makes an ethical difference. It is not satisfied with getting people saved as if the gospel were a spiritual life insurance policy. It goes on to work out our salvation "with fear and trembling, for it is God who works in [us] to will and to act according to his good purpose" (Phil 2:12-13).

The work of spiritual direction outlined by James is more down to earth than the mega-projects of Christian organizations and the professional agendas of executive pastors. It does not lend itself to publicity and promotion. It remains unpretentious and patient, but it makes the difference between life and death.

The Art of Diagnosis

James has been calling attention to things in the lives of his brothers and sisters that they would just as soon ignore. He is not so much a deep thinker as he is perceptive and discerning. He takes the small, ordinary things of life and examines them in the light of the wisdom of God. In our eyes, the poor man in the corner and the lonely widow are simply facts of life to be observed, not changed. James, however, seeks to change the sinful status quo by offering an education in what it means to "wander from the truth." He forcefully describes the wandering in practical terms that cannot easily be denied. He names the evil. He outlines the spiritual sicknesses of favoritism, self-deception, dead faith, slander, judgmentalism, opinionated teaching, hoarding, double-mindedness. This prophet-pastor not only fights against sin, but gives positive steps toward spiritual health.

James's ability to diagnose sin and prescribe a cure reminds me of a physical examination I received in my senior year of high school. I thought I was in perfect health, but I needed a routine check-up and a doctor's signature to attend college. Dr. Eisenberg was friendly and casual. Among his queries about allergies and broken bones, he mixed in a few questions about my college plans.

Five minutes into the exam, I remember thinking, *This guy sure is thorough.* He listened to my heart, thumped my back, checked my reflexes, gently probed my abdomen. When he checked my testicles, he noticed that one of them had a lump. I knew about it, but hadn't given it a second thought because it never hurt. He dropped his casual demeanor immediately and grew noticeably concerned. I realized that he thought something was seriously wrong. Within minutes he had scheduled me to see a specialist. A week later I had major surgery for a malignant tumor that had begun to spread.

My outward appearance and healthy feeling during that routine exam concealed a life-threatening problem. A lazy or incompetent doctor might have missed it. If he had judged me by appearance or accepted my own self-analysis, I probably would not be alive today. In the ordinary, daily routine of doing his job conscientiously, Dr. Eisenberg was instrumental in saving my life.

I picture James serving the church in a similar way as prophet-pastor. His down-to-earth counsel, shaped by the wisdom of God, deals with the sin that threatens the spiritual life of the church. As a physician of the soul, he exposes sin that may not even concern us, and orders surgery that we would never imagine to be necessary. He is thorough and methodical, unwilling to take spiritual health for granted. He does not delight in finding problems and taking measures to fight the disease, but he knows that shunning his responsibility to do so amounts to spiritual malpractice. Lives are on the line. If he can bring someone back to the truth and help restore their spiritual health, his hard work will be rewarded.

Recently I talked with a brother in Christ who had committed adultery a number of years ago. Though he had personally repented and sought God's forgiveness, he had never confessed publicly to doing anything wrong. Many people were aware of his sin, but few knew how he felt about what he had done. Understandably, this led some

Christians to doubt his spiritual integrity. When I shared this with him, he defended his privacy. "Who would I express my repentance to?" he asked. "No one in the church ever told me that I needed to confess and repent openly. They just ignored me."

At a critical point in this man's life, he needed a caring Christian friend to tell him clearly and firmly that his adultery was wrong. Instead, the church let him pursue his sinful course without ever challenging him with the truth. Perhaps so many people question the moral and spiritual authenticity of the church because we do not practice the demanding, sometimes painful art of spiritual direction. We need people who will help us to "work out our salvation with fear and trembling" (Phil 2:12).

The Unfinished Work of Christ

The finished work of Christ reminds us of the unfinished work of spiritual direction. It is precisely because of Christ's gift of salvation by grace that we have a job to do. If God were not working in us to will and to act according to his good purpose, spiritual direction would be pointless. We would have no foundation to build on, no truth to guide us. We would be like a farmer without sunshine and water; we would not even have land or seed. Every ounce of energy invested in spiritual direction depends upon the finished work of Christ. We cannot add to what Christ accomplished through the cross and the resurrection, but we can participate in his work. The finished work of Christ needs to be applied and worked out in our lives. What God's grace has begun, it seeks to finish in the life of every believer. Spiritual direction is an ongoing work of grace within the body of Christ to preserve the integrity and vitality of the Christian life.

James not only concludes by expressing the purpose of his spiritual direction, but calls us to the same task. His hope is that we will begin to serve others the way he has served us. We are to become like our spiritual director—bold in our commitment to the truth, passionate in our concern for others and fervent in the work of prayer. If James could write, "Elijah was a man just like us," we can also say that James was a man just like us—an ordinary servant of Jesus Christ who earnestly sought to turn sinners away from their error. According to James, we *are* our "brother's keeper." Anyone who sees a brother or sister wandering from the truth has the responsibility to help restore that believer to God and to the Christian community. We are entrusted with the shared responsibility of offering spiritual direction.

Spiritual direction is also part of what it means to be a "priesthood of believers." We cannot shirk the responsibility of exercising pastoral care if we are indeed "a chosen people, a royal priesthood, a holy nation, a people belonging to God" (1 Pet 2:9). We are to become like James to one another so that we might declare the praises of God, who called us out of darkness into his wonderful light.

The purpose of spiritual direction is not to tattle on other people. Spiritual guides do not become Dobermans of righteousness, viciously attacking those who stray from the truth. Unfortunately, churches seem to have their share of such people, who confuse the work of Christ with the role of the Pharisee. As the jaundiced see everything as yellow, so the Pharisees found evil in everything Jesus did. When he healed a man's hand, he was breaking the Sabbath. When he taught the Word of God, he undermined their authority. When he cleansed the temple, he was violent. When he drove out demons, he was of the devil. The Pharisees twisted everything Jesus did in order to condemn it.

Søren Kierkegaard described the person whose "eye is alert and trained, not for the understanding of truth, hence for untruth; consequently his sight is prejudiced more and more so that, increasingly defiled, he sees evil in everything, impurity even in what is purest. . . . At last there are no limits to his discovery; for now he discovers sin even when he himself knows that there is none; he discovers it by the help of backbiting, slander, the fabrication of lies, in which he has trained himself so long that he at last believes it. Such a man has verily discovered the multitude of sins!"[1]

Our job is not to *discover* a multitude of sins, but to "*cover over* a multitude of sins" (5:20). At first glance the phrase may sound like James is condoning a cover-*up*. But those receiving his spiritual direction understood the term as referring to atonement, not concealment. At its core, all spiritual direction depends on the atoning sacrifice of Christ. Old Testament priests covered the altar with the blood of goats and lambs. By faith Israel humbly depended upon God's mercy to blot out their sins. As David wrote, "Blessed is he whose transgressions are forgiven, whose sins are covered" (Ps 32:1). The sacrifices prescribed in the Old Testament were "pointers" to help the people of God understand and gratefully receive the redemptive work of Christ. True spiritual direction never forgets the basic work of repentance, confession and humility. Everything we do revolves around the cross of Christ and the gift of forgiveness, acceptance and reconciliation with our God.

Throughout this brief epistle, James has shown us the meaning of salvation in ordinary, daily life. He has brought faith down to earth and told us how to nurture authentic, heartfelt righteousness. We learn to live the Christian faith as it was meant to be lived, to be who Christ intended us to be. We gain a deeper appreciation of the necessity of spiritual direction. We realize that the Christian life does not take shape automatically; we need help to develop perseverance, to overcome bad faith, to tame the tongue and to draw near to God. We need to hold one another accountable to pursue biblical friendship, patient endurance and social justice. We need to accept the challenge to work out the finished work of Christ and "cover over a multitude of sins."

In the book of James we have found practical, relevant, true spiritual direction for our lives. And in the person of James, we have discovered a model to emulate as we strive to become true spiritual directors for others. May we continue to follow the path on which he has led us, from sinful habits to faithful practice, from confusion to clarity, from immaturity to maturity.

Notes

Chapter 2: From Public Relations to Spiritual Direction
[1]G. K. Chesterton, *Orthodoxy* (New York: Image Books, 1959), p. 31.

Chapter 3: From False Expectations to Peace and Joy
[1]See Eugene Peterson, *Answering God* (San Francisco: Harper & Row, 1989), p. 107.
[2]Peter H. Davids, *James* (Grand Rapids: Eerdmans, 1982), p. 73.

Chapter 4: From Self-Pity to Humility
[1]Philip Yancey, *Disappointment with God* (Grand Rapids: Zondervan, 1988), pp. 22-23.
[2]Peter H. Davids, *The Epistle of James* (Grand Rapids: Eerdmans, 1982), p.33.
[3]Ibid., p. 77.
[4]Eugene Peterson, *Answering God* (San Francisco: Harper & Row, 1989), p. 122.

Chapter 5: From Performance to Worship
[1]Lewis B. Smedes, *Mere Morality* (Grand Rapids: Eerdmans, 1983), p. 214.
[2]Margaret Atwood, *The Handmaid's Tale* (New York: Fawcett Crest, 1985), p. 74.
[3]Alec Motyer, *The Message of James* (Downers Grove: InterVarsity Press, 1985), p. 66.
[4]Ibid.
[5]Eugene Peterson, *A Long Obedience in the Same Direction* (Downers Grove: InterVarsity Press, 1980), p. 39.

Chapter 6: From Favoritism to Friendship
[1]Dietrich Bonhoeffer, trans. by John W. Doberstein, *Life Together* (New York: Harper & Row, 1954), pp. 31, 27.
[2]Ibid., p. 26.
[3]Rodney Clapp, "The Celebration of Friendship," *Reformed Journal* (August 1989), p. 13.

Chapter 7: From Bad Faith to Saving Faith
[1]See John Stott, *The Spirit, the Church & the World* (Downers Grove: InterVarsity Press, 1990), p. 314.
[2]Dietrich Bonhoeffer, *The Cost of Discipleship* (New York: Macmillan, 1963), pp. 55, 47-48.
[3]See Donald G. Bloesch, *Essentials of Evangelical Theology*, Vol. 1 (San Francisco: Harper & Row, 1978), pp. 223-52.
[4]Eugene H. Peterson, *The Contemplative Pastor* (Waco: Christianity Today/Word, 1989), p. 17.

Chapter 8: From Opinion to Truth
[1]Harry Blamires, *The Christian Mind* (London, S.P.C.K, 1963), p. 107.

Chapter 9: From Confusion to Understanding
[1]C. S. Lewis, *Mere Christianity* (New York: Macmillan, 1960), p. 167.
[2]Peter H. Davids, *James* (Grand Rapids: Eerdmans, 1982), p. 151.

Chapter 10: From Conflict to Peace
[1]Larry Crabb, *Inside Out* (Colorado Springs: Navpress, 1988), pp. 34-35.
[2]Alec Motyer, *The Message of James* (Downers Grove: InterVarsity Press, 1985), p. 141.
[3]Ibid., p. 145.
[4]John White, *Flirting with the World* (Wheaton: Harold Shaw, 1982), pp. 28-29.
[5]Michael Marshall, quoted in George Gallup, Jr., "Secularism and Religion: Trends in Contemporary America," *Emerging Trends* 10 (December 1987): 3.

Chapter 11: From Presumption to Submission
[1]Daniel Boorstin, *The Discoverers* (New York: Random House, 1983), p. 86.
[2]See Donald B. Kraybill and Phyllis Pellman Good, eds., *Perils of Professionalism: Essays on Christian Faith and Professionalism* (Scottdale, Penn.: Herald Press, 1982).

[3]John Perkins, A *Quiet Revolution* (Waco, Tex.: Word, 1976), p. 35.
[4]Eugene Peterson, A *Long Obedience in the Same Direction* (Downers Grove: InterVarsity Press, 1980), p. 116.

Chapter 12: From Self-Interest to Service

[1]Charles Colson, "Living in the New Dark Ages," *Christianity Today*, October 20, 1989, p. 32.
[2]Daniel Yankelovich, *New Rules: Searching for Self-Fulfillment in a World Turned Upside Down* (New York: Random House, 1981), p. 189.

Chapter 13: From Passivity to Patience

[1]Eugene H. Peterson, *Reversed Thunder* (San Francisco: Harper & Row, 1988), p. 94.

Chapter 14: From Complexity to Simplicity

[1]John R. W. Stott, *Christian Counter-Culture* (Downers Grove: InterVarsity Press, 1978), p. 102.
[2]See John Stott, *Christian Mission in the Modern World* (Downers Grove: InterVarsity Press, 1975), pp. 29-30.
[3]Alec Motyer, *The Message of James* (Downers Grove: InterVarsity Press, 1985), pp. 206-7.

Chapter 15: From Grand Designs to Basic Commitments

[1]Søren Kierkegaard, *Works of Love*, cited in A *Kierkegaard Anthology*, ed. Robert Bretall (Princeton, N.J.: Princeton University Press, 1946), p. 312.